FALL 2019
ISSUE 18

letter from the editor

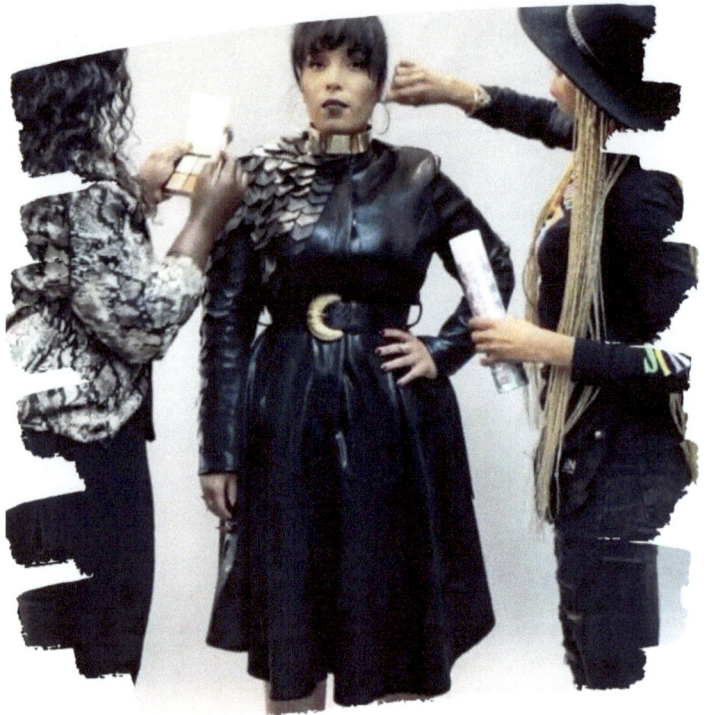

AThis issue was a little hectic this to you such a complex and heavy schedule. However, autumn time is my favorite time of the year. There's nothing better than a crisp smell of apple pie and pumpkin spice latte to warm your heart. The layers , scarfs, autumn colors and mustard. Provides me with a warm sense of validation for the holidays. This feature issue we highlighted Jela a former Bad Girls Club member on Oxygen network. Jela is now converted into a supermodel. Not only was she amazing And the epitome of extraordinary

She was such a divine light to work with.From the exceptional designer to the glam squad the vision was carried into such a vast piece of artwork I hope you guys all enjoyed the creative vision at the Fashion Gxd Magazines that has put forward for this falls issue. With much love

Pilar Scratch
EDITOR IN CHIEF

CONTENTS

NEW CLOTHING
AMOT APPERAL

Ready- set- go! New clothing for a new season , gearing up for the atumn trends.

INTERVIEW
QUINCY CHAD

Starz Hit show "Power" break out star talks preparatin and owning his own power.

THE SKY IS THE LIMIT
EXPLORING BOOKS

innovative books for the approaching holiday season that make awesome stocking stuffers

COVER INTERVIEW
JELA (COVER STORY)

Former Bad Girls Club member has made a big splash in the modeling world causing her fame to heighten beyond a reality tv star.

IN MEDIA
YELLA RAY

the princess of media shares her top secrets of success in the busy cncerete ungle of new york city

INTERVIEW
JAZZ NATURALS

new products fresh for fall best for accessorizing

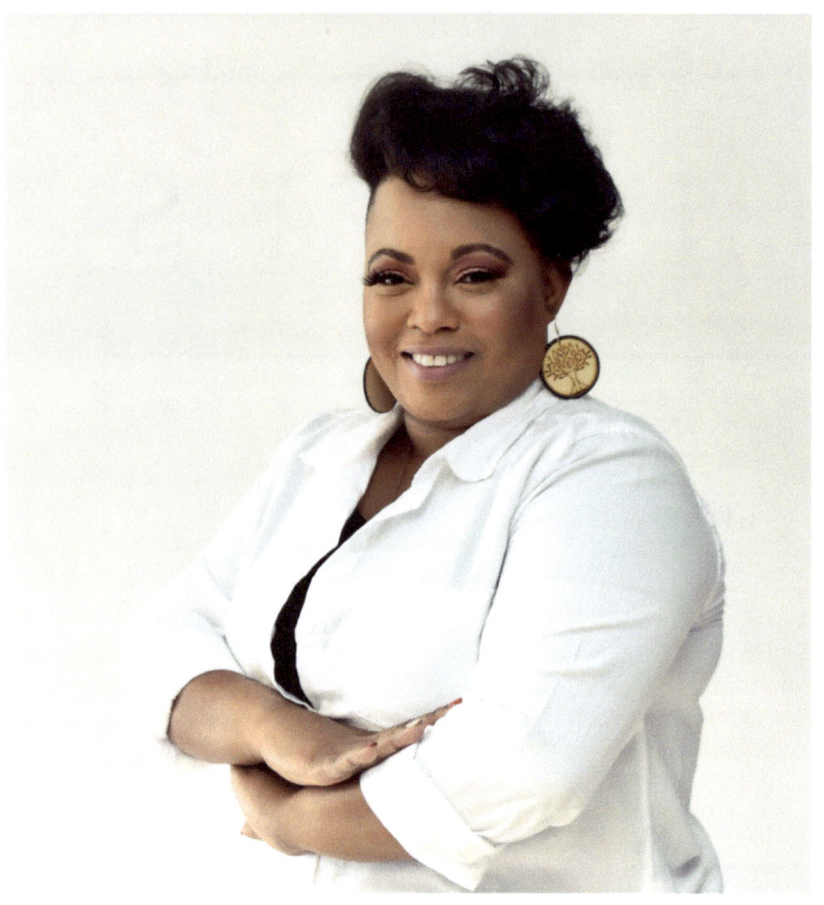
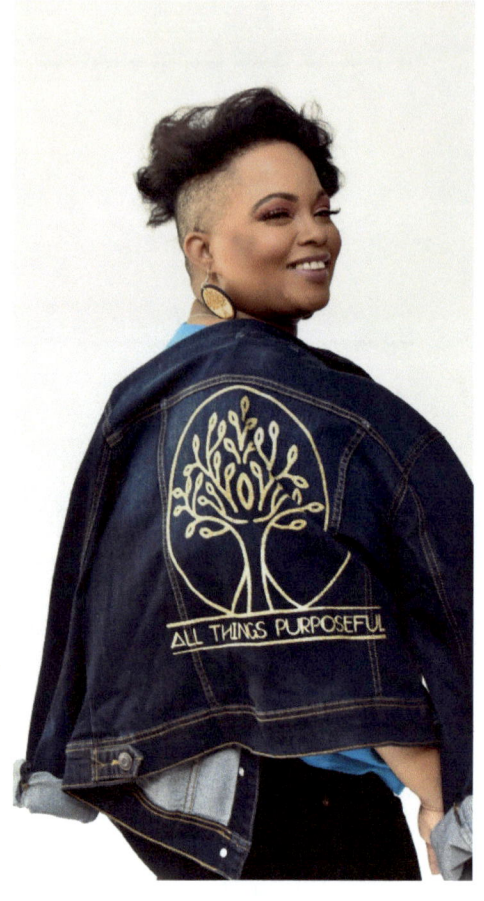

All Things Purposeful The Brand Of Inspiration

EDITED BY : JOANA SMITH

All things Purposeful is both a clothing and consulting company. We assist individuals on their journey to owning their own business and We offer apparel that spreads messages of encouragement.

**Social media accounts:
Facebook: All Things Purposeful Instagram: AllThingsPurposeful8 Twitter: AllPurposeful
www.allthingspurposeful.com**

Natasha N. Denson, she is the CEO of All Things Purposeful. Natasha was born, raised, and educated in East Orange, NJ. During her grammar, middle and high school education she always had earthly angels who were there to look after her. She is a survivor of Child abuse and sexual abuse. In her recent life storm when she hit rock bottom, she learned that God was using her pain to push her into her purpose. Thus, All Things Purposeful was born. With her brand, she hopes to inspire and encourage others to use the gifts that they were given to complete their purpose while here on earth.

THE PURPOSE SECTION

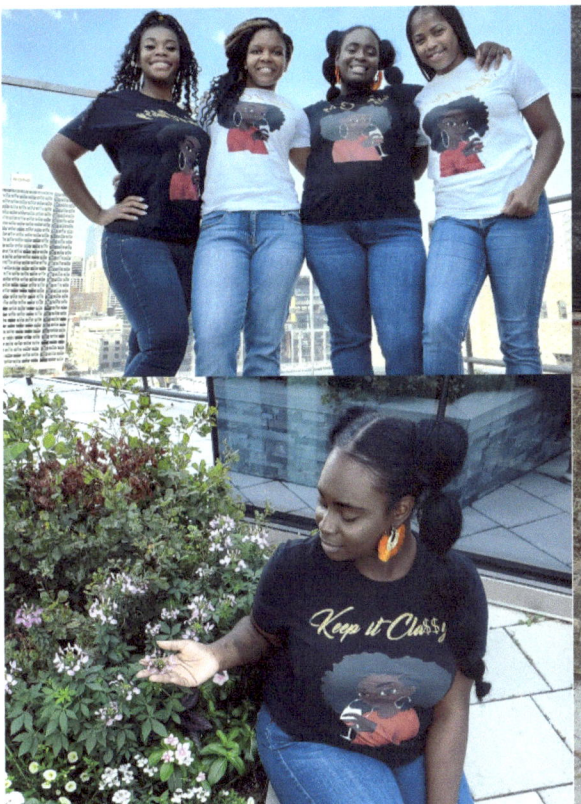
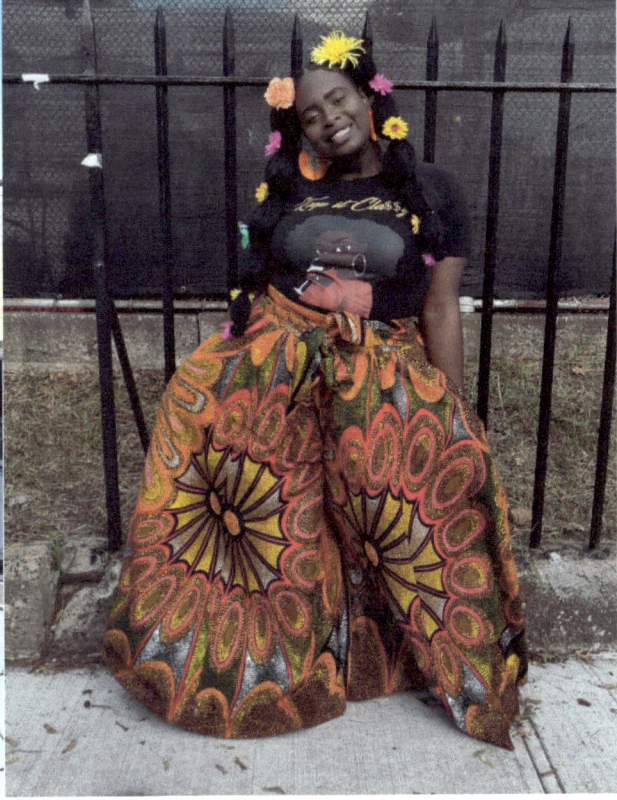

KEEP IT CLA$$Y

is a brand developed by Shadiqua Smith-Spann to help raise money to establish a community center in Philadelphia, Pennsylvania. The community center will provide Mental Health resources with an emphasis on the challenges of African American people. Her passion for the mental health field over the course of 4 years has given birth to the idea of opening the center. Shadiqua's journey began with her own experiences and mental health struggles. Throughout her life, she has withstood numerous traumatic events. Being as a suicide survivor and was hospitalized several times during her upbringing is a testament to these events. The concept of mental health is misunderstood and often ignored in her hometown.

When discussing her experiences with friends and family, she felt that nobody wanted to confront their own thoughts and feelings on the topic of mental health. As a result, she identifies the shroud of stigma revolving around mental health in the black community as a greater cause for concern. When she tried to reach out for help through the mental health system, she realized not only was it difficult to navigate but practitioners were culturally insensitive to some of the struggles a person of color endured. There were many moments where she felt the therapist was struggling to understand her.

The mental health system discouraged her from getting the help she needed since it's methods caused her more trauma. When she reflected on the mental health system, she realized that there were three different groups in need of support.

The first group wants to receive support but does not know where to start. The second group has received support in the past but didn't find it beneficial. Lastly, the third group is too afraid to seek support overall. Shadiqua was apart of all three groups in different stages of her life which allow her to empathise with its members. Shadiqua has been through a lot of trials and tribulations not only dealing with her own mental health but supporting others as well. Shadiqua's desire to encourage these groups influenced her to become a Certified Peer Specialist or CPS.

A CPS is someone who was diagnosed with a serious mental illness and is licensed to support a peer that struggles with mental illness. Her experience and credentials are one of the main reasons why she's passionate about opening up a community center. Shadiqua's vision for the community center is that it will be a place where anyone is welcome to receive resources and share their stories or feelings free of judgment. She wants people to feel safe, bold, free, and experience a sense of belonging. Once they are ready, the community center will be a hub guiding people towards a successful recovery.

GOAL TO RAISE FUNDS

Not only is it Keep It Cla$$y's goal to raise funds to establish the community center, but the shirt itself has a meaning to it. The slogan was inspired by a conversation with Shadiqua's boyfriend. The original idea was "keep it classy and drink wine." The slogan evolved into "Keep it Cla$$y" as it stands to remind women of color to maintain their wealth and dignity. Shadiqua wanted to also make the shirt personal. Growing up as a "dark-skinned" woman exposed her to discrimination. It made her hate her own skin. With time, she learned how to love herself despite what society preferences. Shadiqua wants to share the importance of self-love and self-respect with those who went through similar experiences. "Dark skin women are dope," said Shadiqua during our interview. The glass of wine and hoop earrings reflects Shadiqua's wine so she had to make sure that was in the shirt, and she loves her hoops. "Hoops goes with every outfit" she said. In addition, she had to represent the natural hair, to make the shirt all the way black girl magic style. Shadiqua started building her brand 4 months ago, and don't plan on stopping. You can find her on Instagram @_keepitclassy or her website at www.keepitclassy.org

FALL 2019 | LIFESTYLE EDITION

Getting To Know Amot Apparel

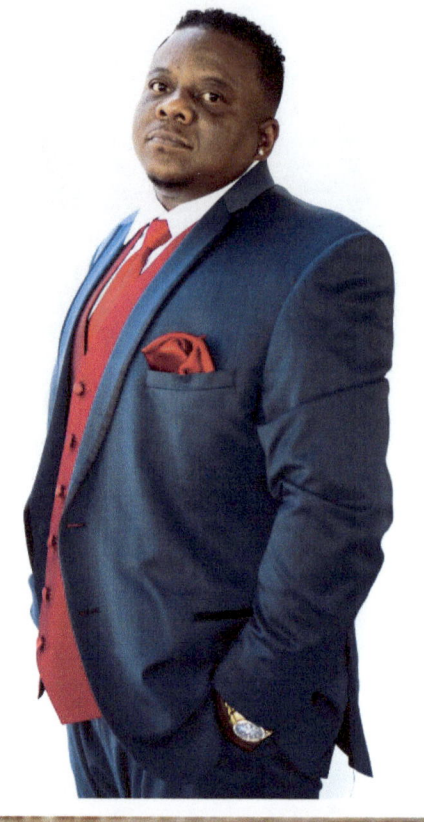

Amot Apparel, which is an abbreviation of "A Matter of Time", is an urban casual and sports brand established in California in 2016. Amot Apparel caters to the entertainment industry and brings all fresh original designs to center stage.

FIVE WAYS TO BECOME SUCCESSFUL:

Believe in your product, Set goals and be consistent, Know your competitor and try to out work them, Be passionate about what you do, Networking

SOCIAL MEDIA HANDLES:

Instagram.com/AmotApparel
Facebook.com/AmotApparel
Snapchat/ I Am_AmotApparel
Twitter/ Founder@ AmotApparel

WWW.AMOTAPPAREL.COM

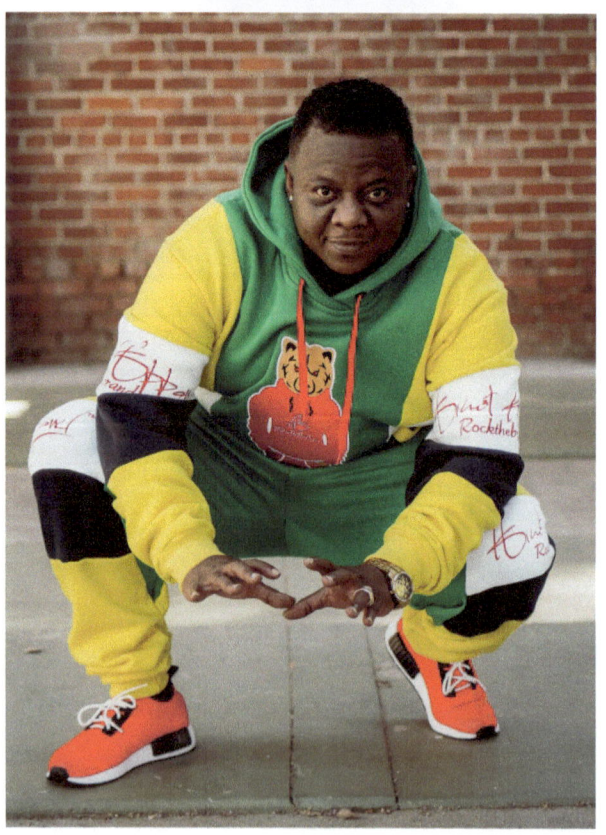

LIFESTYLE | FALL 2019

" Exclusive Interview

What does Amot stand for? Amot is an abbreviation for "A Matter of Time".

How did you come up with the name Amot? I came up with the name Amot at the age of 16 when my mother passed on, although at the time I knew I wanted to own a clothing brand, I could never come up with a name. I was sketching one day in a somewhat depressed state and thinking about my mother and said it's just "A Matter of Time" before I see you again and there it was Amot.

Did you ever see yourself where you are now? Not to sound cocky but yes, this is my passion and my vision was clear of where I wanted to be so I dedicated the work and time needed to see it through.

How did you get started? I started by distributing clothing out of my car to the locals in the neighborhood. How long has the brand been in business? 3 years

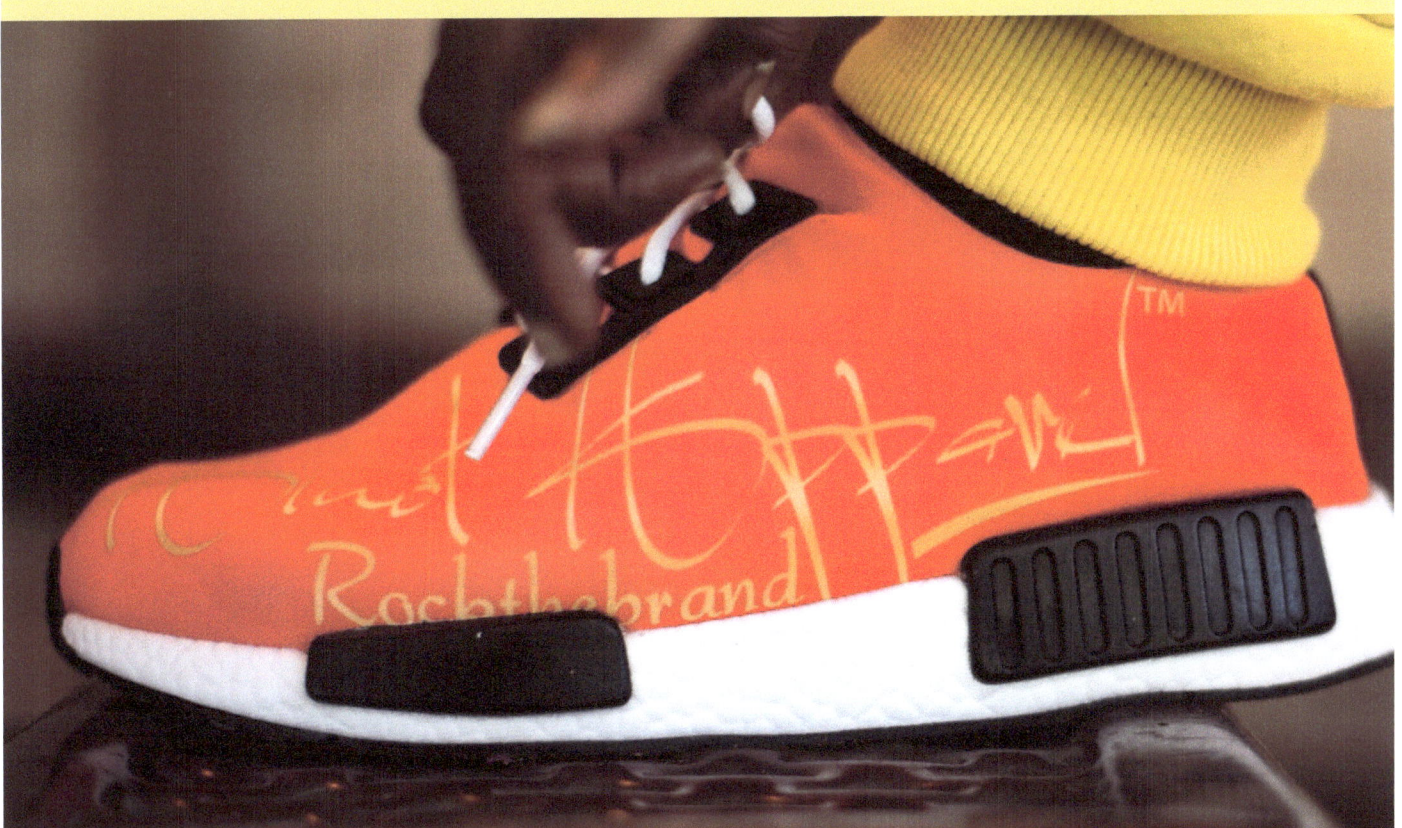

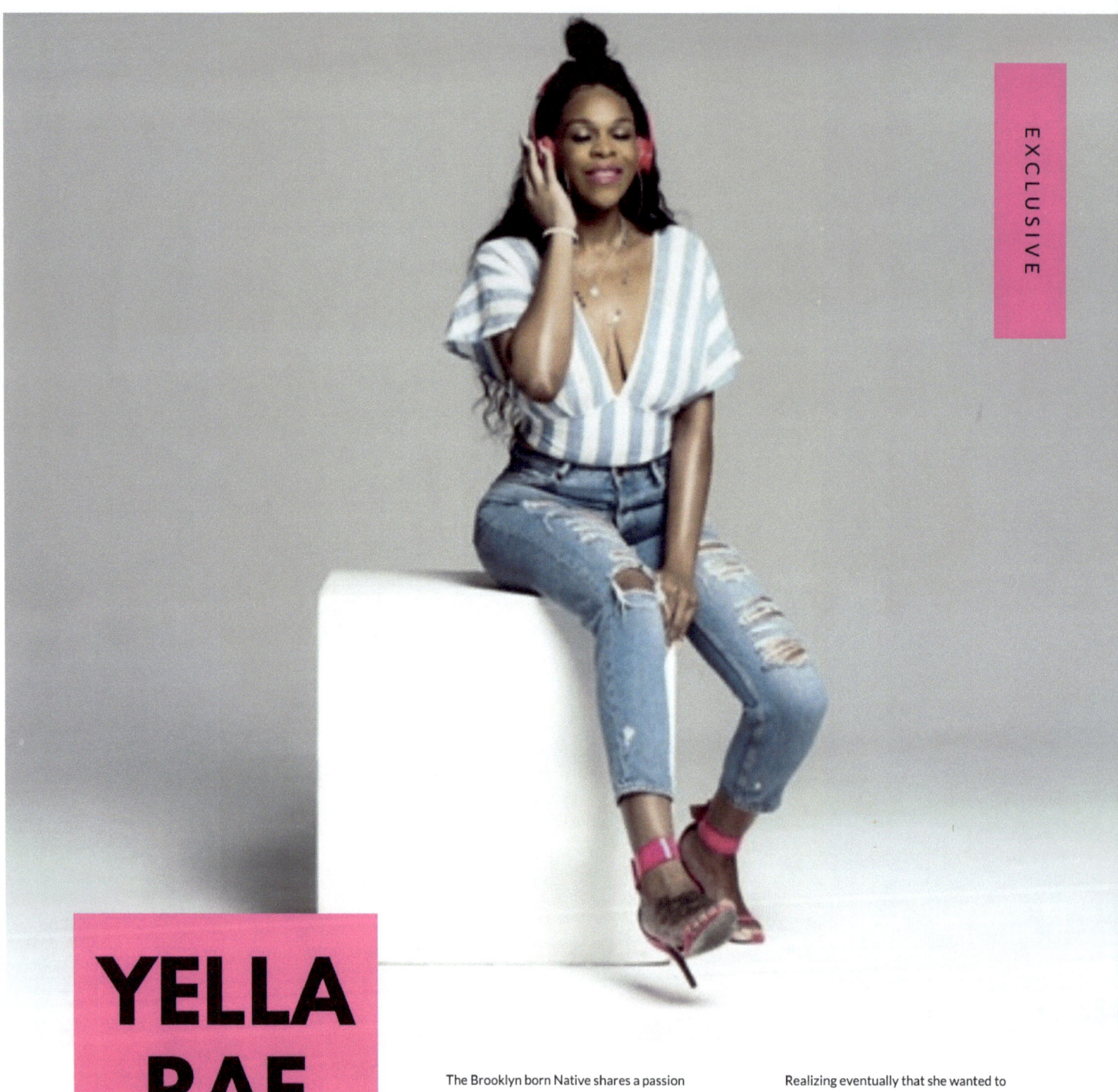

EXCLUSIVE

YELLA RAE

"I want young girls to know that giving up should never be an option despite negative influences and setbacks of the world. LIVE YOUR DREAMS!
-Yella Rae

WRITTEN BY : @VINTAGELIPGLOSS
PUBLICIST : EVB @VINTAGELIPGLOSS" EGHAREVBA

The Brooklyn born Native shares a passion for hip-hop and entertainment journalism, that of which has lead her to her current career as a radio show personality. The enthusiastic and great spirited being has shaped success with the passion to overcome adversity. Giving herself the name Yella Rae after many people described her look and beauty to be similar to award winning actress Lisa Rae, the name has stuck ever since. Yella Rae is no stranger to higher learning. She has studied mass communications and media in college where she obtained her passion for radio hosting having her first start in college radio. A woman of many talents, Yella Rae once migrated to California in pursuit of an acting career.

Realizing eventually that she wanted to further her career in journalism, Yella Rae eventually moved back home to NYC. Upon arriving back, she obtained a hosting job as a radio personality at Q96FM (a sister station to 93.5 FM that reaches over 40,000,000 listeners in the tri-state area) where she currently hosts her own show Vocalize NY. A bubbly and inviting personality that sparks the airwaves is a shoe in for good laughs and entertainment on a Yella Rae segment. Yella Rae is in high hopes of furthering her career and remains a walking testimony of overcoming adversity. From overcoming homelessness to a rising commodity, Yella Rae is a true example of strength by any means necessary to achieve your dream.

FIVE SECRETS TO SUCCESS

Consistency, Write Out Your Goals, Have Great Organization, Network, Believe In Yourself

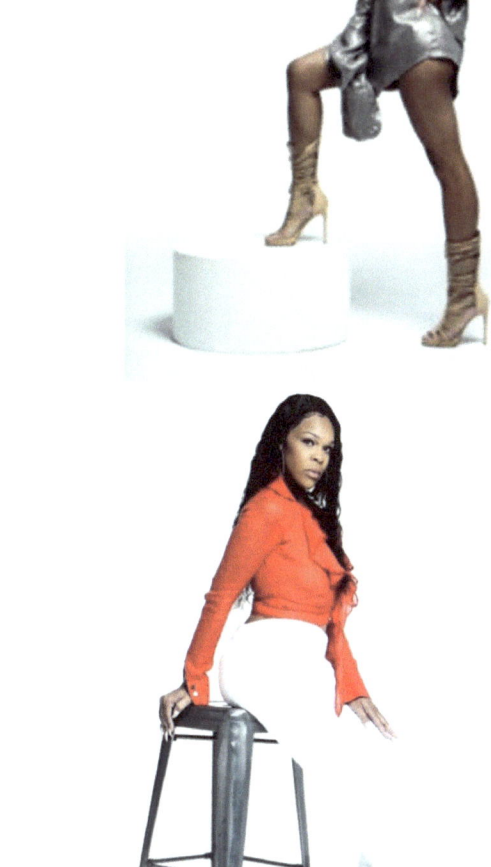

Yella Rae is primarily inspired by the strength that she has obtained through overcoming her own personal adversities. Having days in her life when she didn't even know when she would eat her next meal, living in her car and not having a place to live and scraping up money just to make ends meet is what has pushed this rising sensation to fight to overcome adversity.

The survival game remains a factor that keeps Yella Rae motivated simply to want a better life while achieving her dreams. Similarly, she admires the work ethic of media gurus such as Oprah Winfrey and Wendy Williams who also have astonishing stories of their rise in radio and television. Yella Rae always finds strength in reminiscing on the words of her grandfather who taught her to never give up.

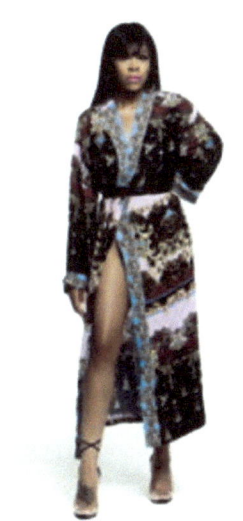

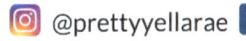 @prettyyellarae 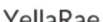 YellaRae

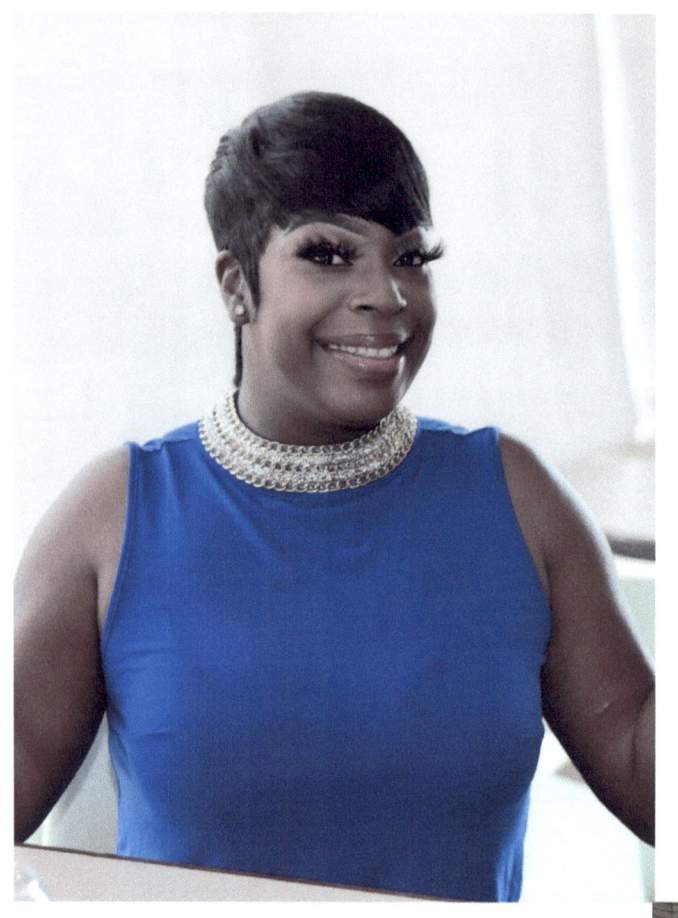

THE CEO'S SECRET WEAPON

Prima Donna was established in 2016 and has been in business for three years in the Albany Georgia area. She has changed over 200 trainees to become technicians through the USA. She's very passionate and knowledgeable in everything she does. Prima Donna is honest and loyal to all of her clients.

She will go the extra mile to please her clientele. If you're looking for an affordable quality service Pima Donna is the way to go.

FIVE TIPS ON BEING A SUCCESSFUL ENTREPRENEUR

- Courageous Faith
- Investment
- Education
- Techniques
- Networking/ Marketing /Branding.

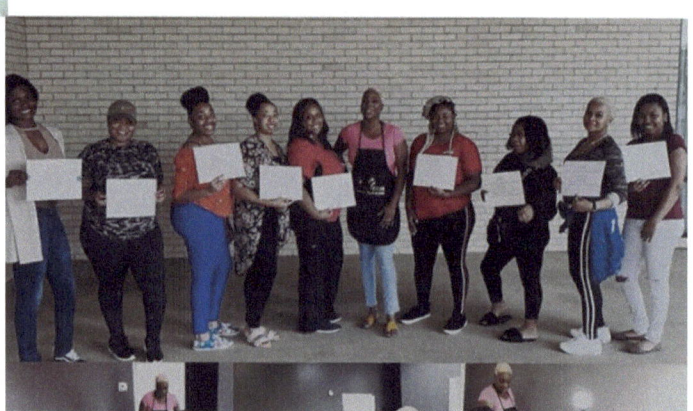

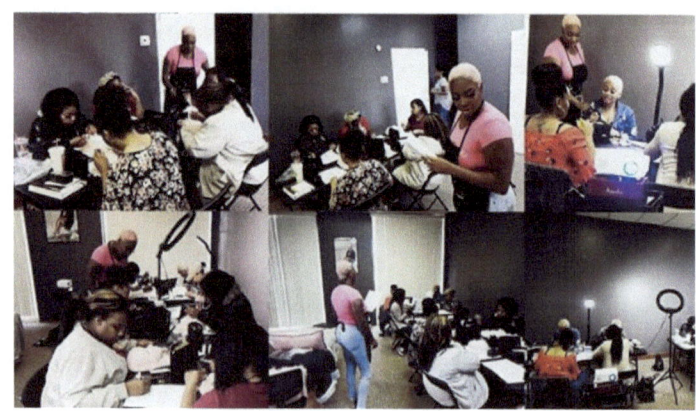

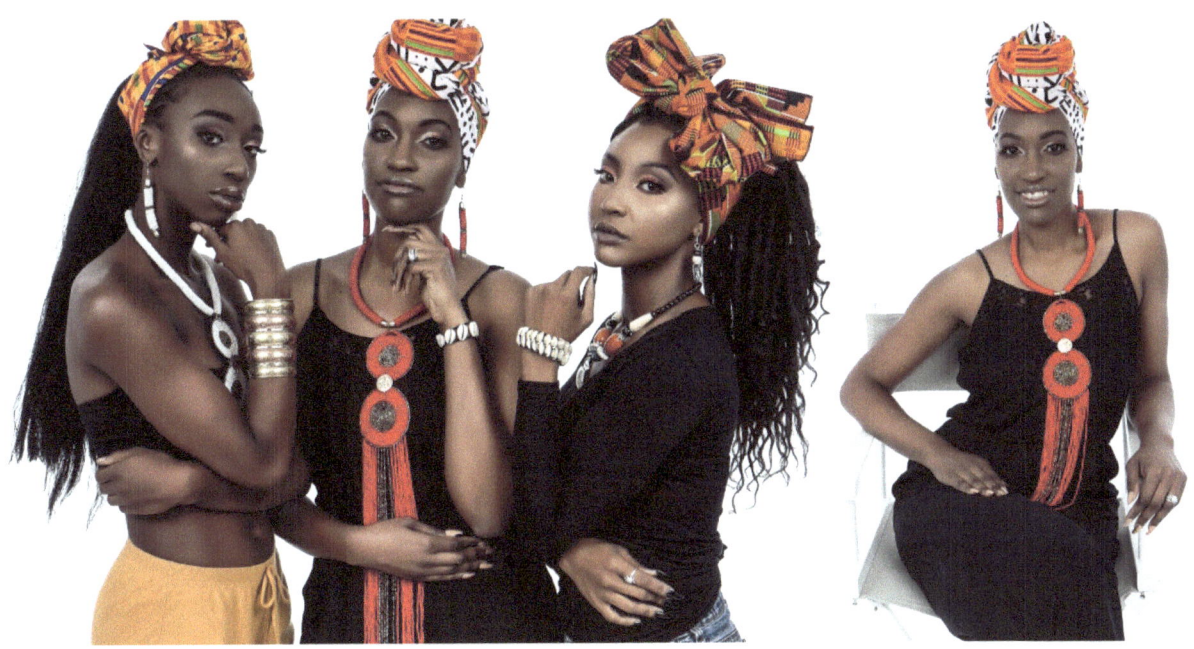

ACCESSORIZING AT ITS FINEST WITH JAZZIE NATURALS

MUA: Desires Design
Photographer: Maurice Orange
Models: Naomi Nalani & Miah Josey

Jazzie Naturals is an accessories brand that offers bold, unique, and urban pieces. Our pieces are here to serve the fashion forward woman. We are committed to our three values; quality, innovative design and product satisfaction. No one wants to wear the same accessories as everyone else; accessories are how we express our individuality. Jazzie Naturals founder Jazell Byars started the brand as a way to encourage women to be their authentic self and express themselves through their accessories. We are Queens, let Jazzie Naturals help you stand out from the crowd.

jazzienaturals.com
Instagram: @jazzie_naturals

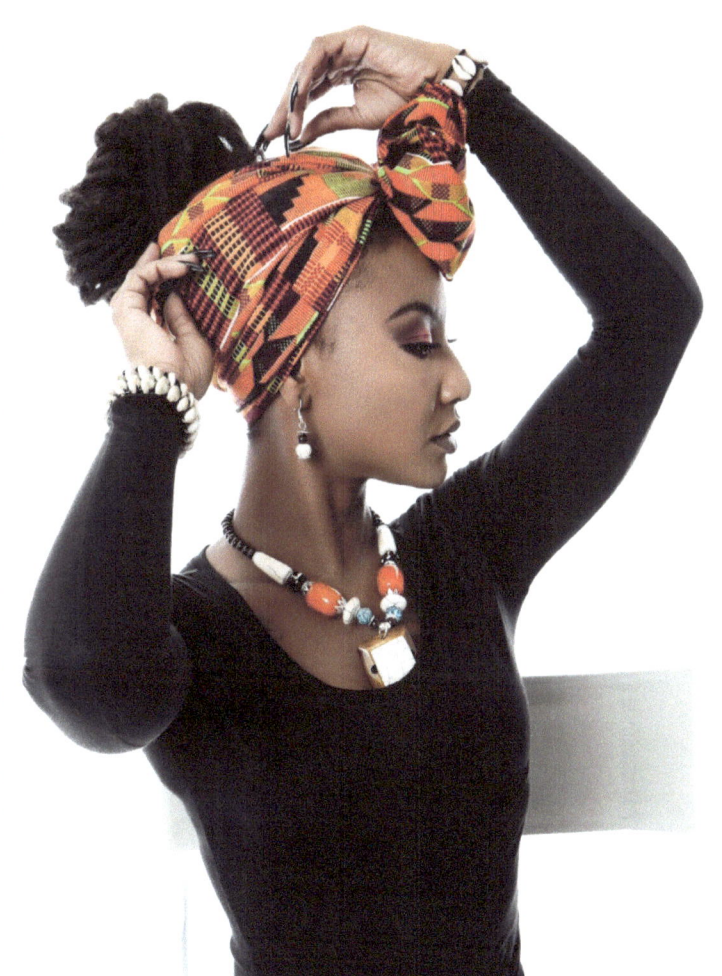

FASHION GXD MAGAZINE																									FALL 2019

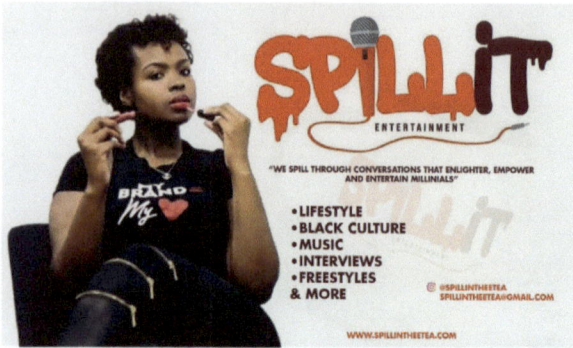

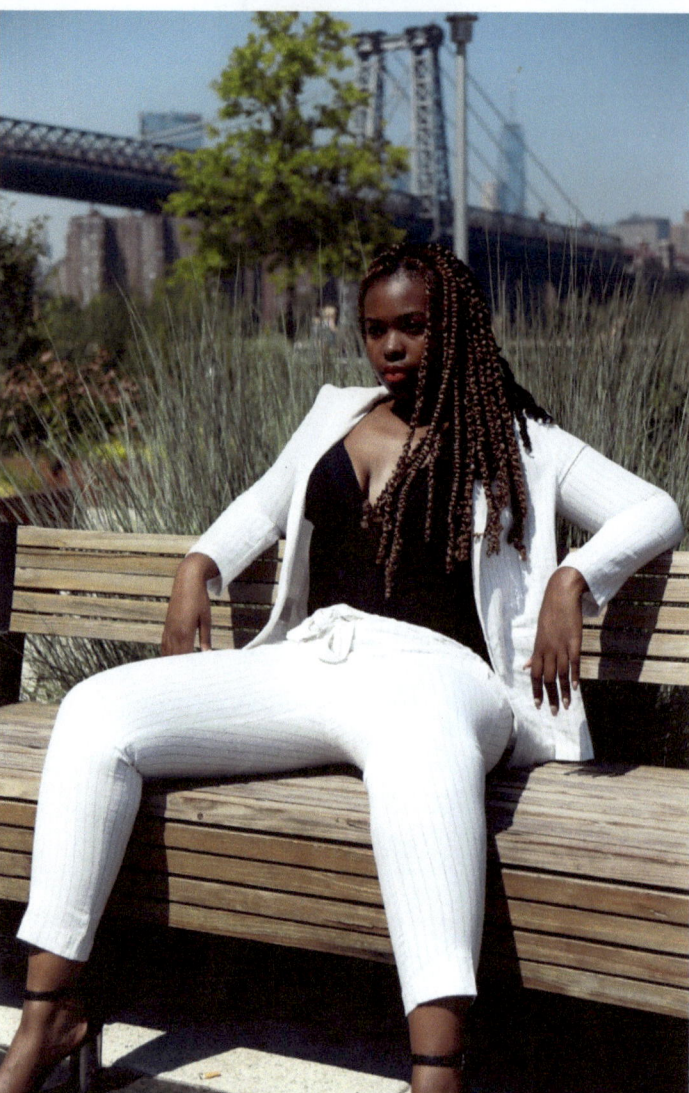

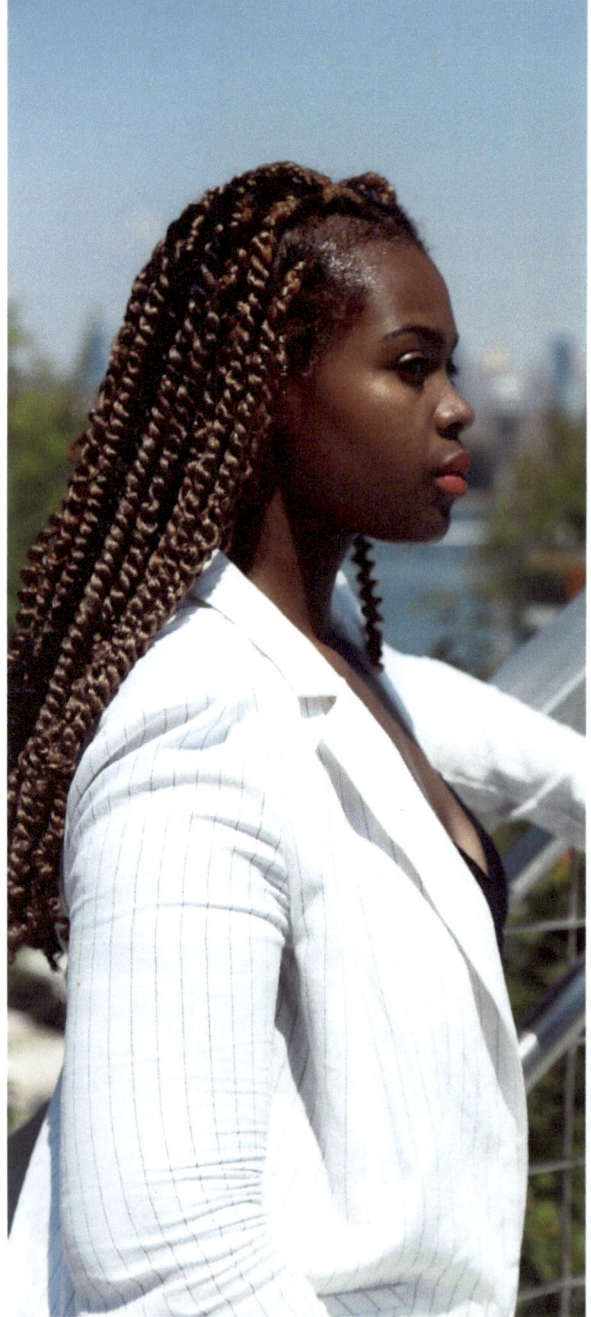

TIPS ON BEING A SUCCESSFUL ENTREPRUER WITH

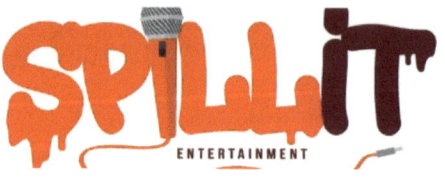

Don't pretend to be someone you're not . Often time people live above their means and below their standards , and that's something I see everyday. . Procrastination is a drug that you should stay away from. I've procrastinated so much that I thought these things would actually get done at the time i needed them to . Your best friends are strangers. From the time I started my own business I noticed I had the most support from strangers . I had two best friends that took them months to even subscribe to my youtube channel and truthfully, none of them even reposted my videos. Don't make putting yourself last a habit. I've spent years putting the emotional and mental needs of others before mine and it when it came time for my break down I was the only one around. Write everything down . Not type , not note , but WRITE. There's something about writing that connects the words from your pen which are ultimately your own thoughts to the universe

FACEBOOK.COM/THEPRETTYHUSTLERR
SPILLINTHEETEA.COM
 INSTAGRAM.COM/SPILLITENT

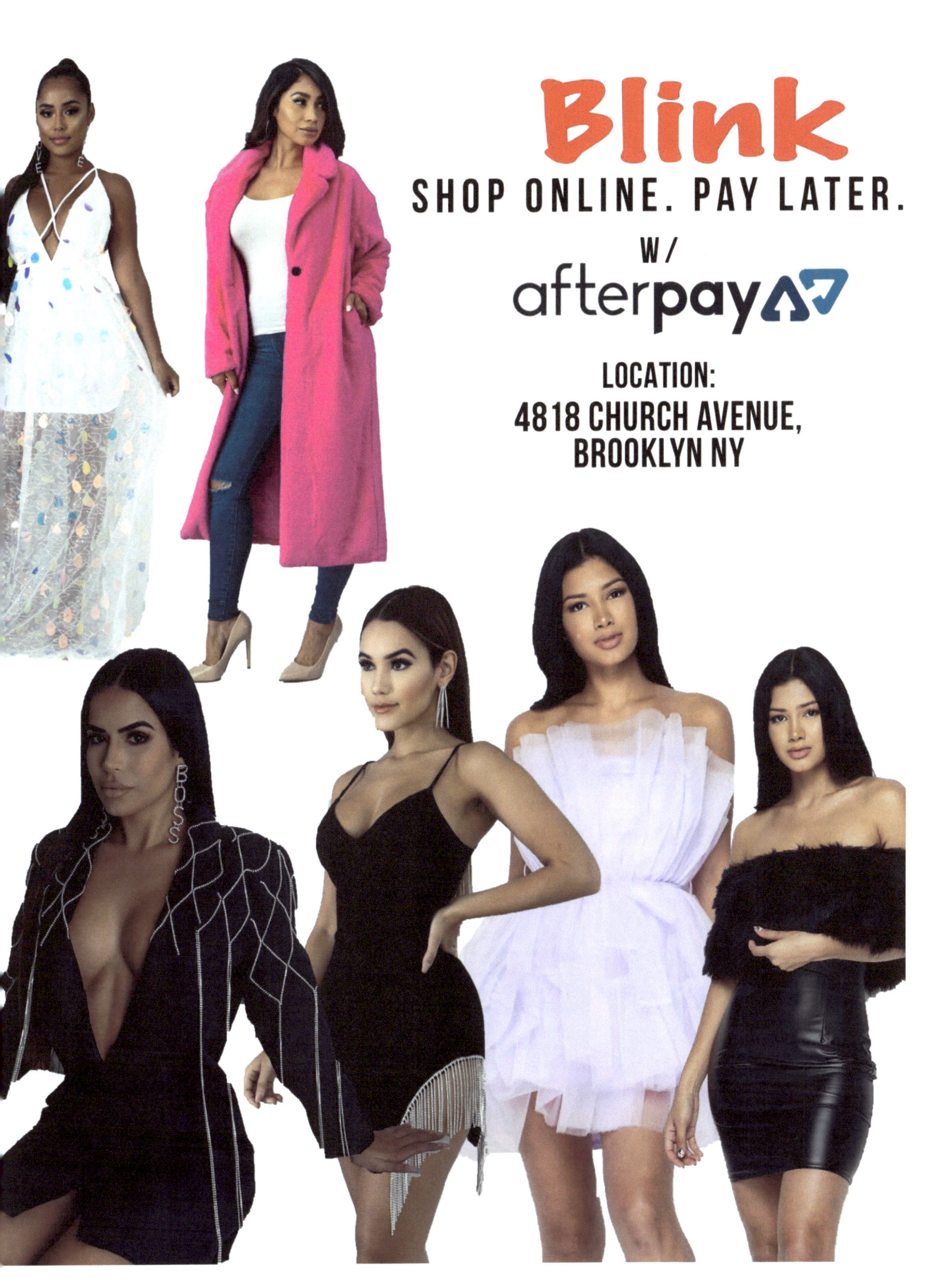

FASHION GXD MAGAZINE   OCT • 2019

FAITH & ENTREPRENUERSHIP COINCIDE WITH OSEREME SAMSON-IBHAGUI

THE MECHANICAL ENGINEERING STUDENTS SELF HELP PODCAST IS HEALING DIVERSE GENERATIONS

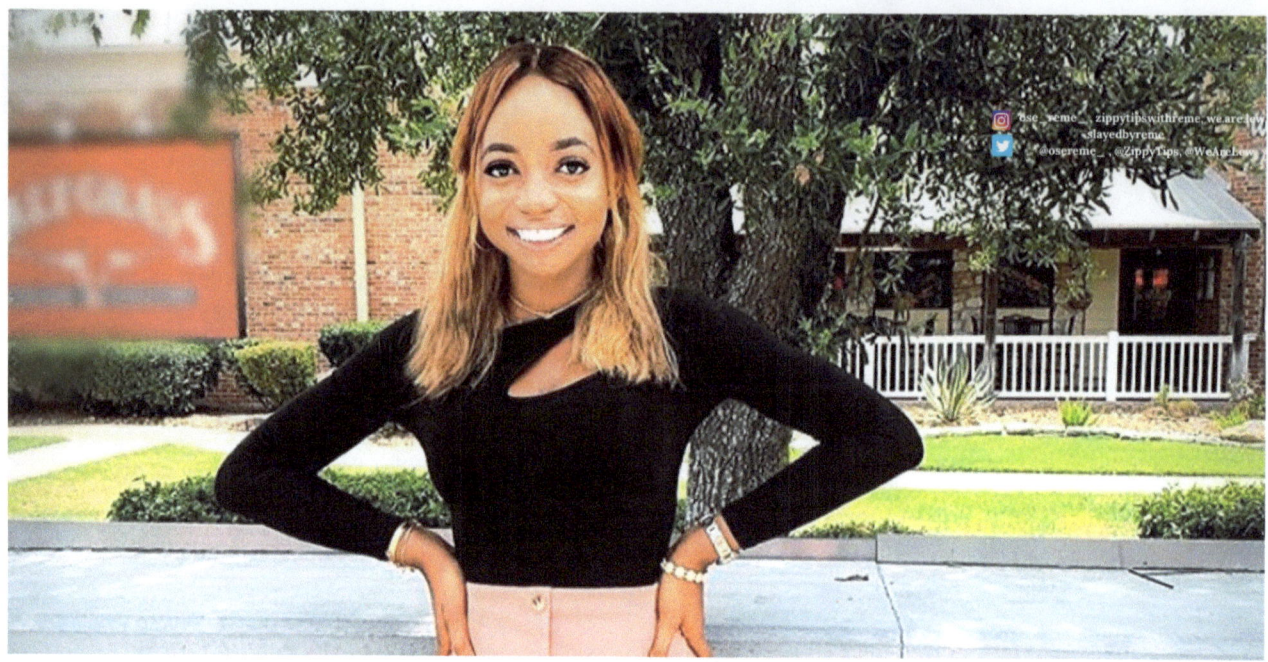

"FAILURE IS A PROCESS OF SUCCESS, PEOPLE THAT AVOID FAILURE ALSO AVOID SUCCESS"

We sat down with an amazing rising entrepreneur Osereme Samson-Ibhagui. Osereme is mostly known as Reme Samson, is a Junior in Mechanical Engineering at the Prairie View A&M University. Her desire to make ladies/women love and appreciate themselves is one of the driving forces for her establishing her non-profit organization, Ladies Empowering the World (L.E.W.). A self-help podcast Zippy Tips with Reme Samson and managing her business Slayed by Reme. She continually places God at the center of it all. Here's our exclusive interview with the rising brand.

Fashion Gxd Magazine : How did the idea for your non profit business come about?

Answer : I believe in empowering women and granting them their rights, and I can be considered a lady activist. There are several disciplines women can be enabled, spiritually, academically, financially, emotionally, mentally and the list goes on, I decided to create an empowerment group with the help of two other amazing ladies that focuses on self-love and spiritual growth. Like the famous saying goes if you see a problem rather than going around talking generate a solution. On my podcast, I usually recommend my listeners to join an organization that could help them in their faith, belief and helps actualize who they want to be. I felt like I was throwing them to the streets without proper guidance, having this organization, I can help keep my listeners focus on their goals.

Fashion Gxd Magazine : How do you find people to bring into your organization that truly care about the organization the way you do?

Answer: It's definitely not easy finding people to bring to your organization or business who would be passionate the same way you are because sometimes people see these opportunities as a way for them to boost their clouts or their resumes, which is totally fine when they are of good intentions. They might not genuinely care for it the way you do I would say one of the essential things I do is actually pray, and I pray that the Holy Spirit guides my decision and actually decides for me rather than me deciding for myself.

Fashion Gxd Magazine : What three pieces of advice would you give to other children who want to become entrepreneurs or commence non profit organizations?

FASHION GXD MAGAZINE
OCT • 2019

/ 2019

HOST OF THE ZIPPY TIPS PODCAST & CO-FOUNDER OF L.E.W

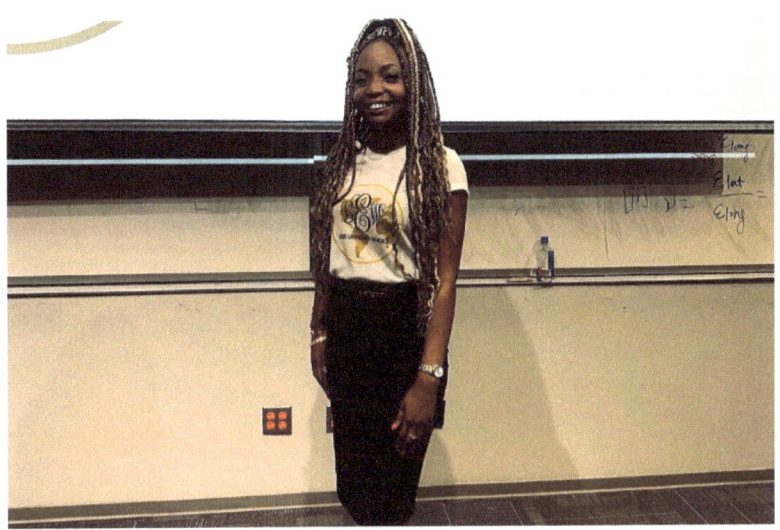

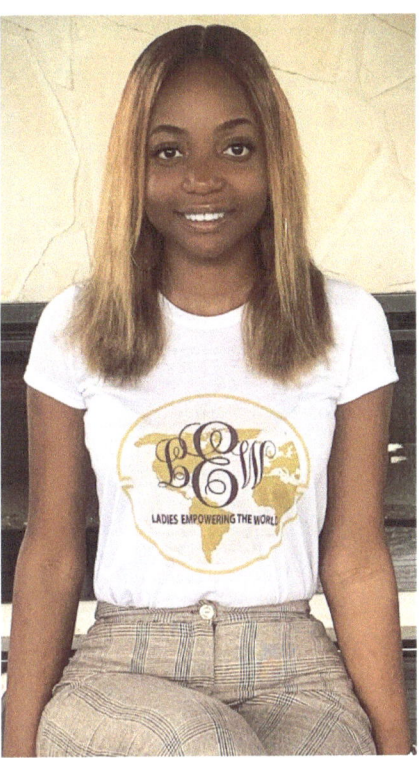

'I BELIEVE IN EMPOWERING WOMEN AND GRANTING THEM THEIR RIGHTS'

Answer: Being an entrepreneur and a co-founder of a non-profit organization, I will give three different advice for both. As an entrepreneur; Be passionate about your new business. Have enough funds(capital) for your business ,Make your product/service available to the right group of audience. For example, opening a grocery store in a residential area will bring more profit than if it were open in a commercial space. As for non-profit organization; Create a purpose/reason and genuinely care about Have a sound support system; for instance, executive board, sponsors Self-care is vital because sometimes you can actually get carried away caring about people and their problems/needs, which really can be detrimental to you. Another advice that works for both is, do not get in competition with anyone, know your worth and stick by it.

.Fashion Gxd Magazine :What would you say are the top three skills needed to be a successful entrepreneur?

Answer: Top three skills needed to be an entrepreneur basically Rightly set your priorities, Create demands for your products and services Effectively communicate through social media or in person.

Fashion Gxd Magazine :What have been some of your failures, and what have you learned from them?

Answer: L.O.L. there is a famous saying that goes failure is a process of success, people that avoid failure also avoid success, so definitely I have experienced failure. Some of the lessons I have learned from my failures include; I do not rely on people for anything,, I avoid unhealthy competitions because sometimes my path and the other person path can be totally opposite and it made me lose focus, I try to live my life not pleasing anyone but God, I stick to being myself. People will always have opinions about me, but I never let that affect me as long as I know who I am, and I understand who I am.

Fashion Gxd Magazine : How many hours do you work a day on average?

Answer:*laughs* I work around the clock, I am a full-time student, I have an organization I need to cater for because it's the first year, I have a podcast I'm trying to reach out to a specific amount of people , I have my own business, I have a social life I need to take care of so I work around the clock there are no particular. However, I try to clear my weekends for a little self-care.

Fashion Gxd Magazine :What motivates you?

Answer: My biggest motivation is my family, my parents have never put me in a situation where I ever had to ask for things twice or has ever prevented me from expressing myself, they have trained me to have self-control but never shut me down. My dad let my mom express herself; however, she wants; he has shown nothing but love to my mom and my siblings, and I'll always be grateful for that. My siblings literally are my strength; they motivate me to be a better individual.

Fashion Gxd Magazine: How do you generate new ideas?

Answer: I generate new ideas by moving out of my comfort zone because whenever I get out of my comfort zone, I get to meet new groups of people with a new mindset, people of different reasoning. Then, I get inspired to think out the box and get myself involved with people of several backgrounds in different ideologies.

Fashion Gxd Magazine : What sacrifices have you had to make to be a successful entrepreneur?

Answer: It's honestly not easy, sometimes I have dedicated sleepless nights to make sure things are actually done, I have spent a crazy amount of money on the spot to make sure I have quality service, sometimes I have to deprive myself of fleshly desires to make sure I'm spiritually right to speak to people and impact their lives, sometimes I have to be absent from some events that I really needed to be present for.

Fashion Gxd Magazine : Where you see yourself and your business in 10 years? 20 years?

Answer: In the next ten years, I see myself as a woman that will fully impact a lot of generations, a philanthropist who has actually helped my country Nigeria and several other African countries, very spiritually inclined with God, a woman of substance and a model to many young ladies around the World. I am a giant and non-destructive force, and there is nothing that can stop me because I am rooted in the right source. I will like to be considered a lady that empowers the World.

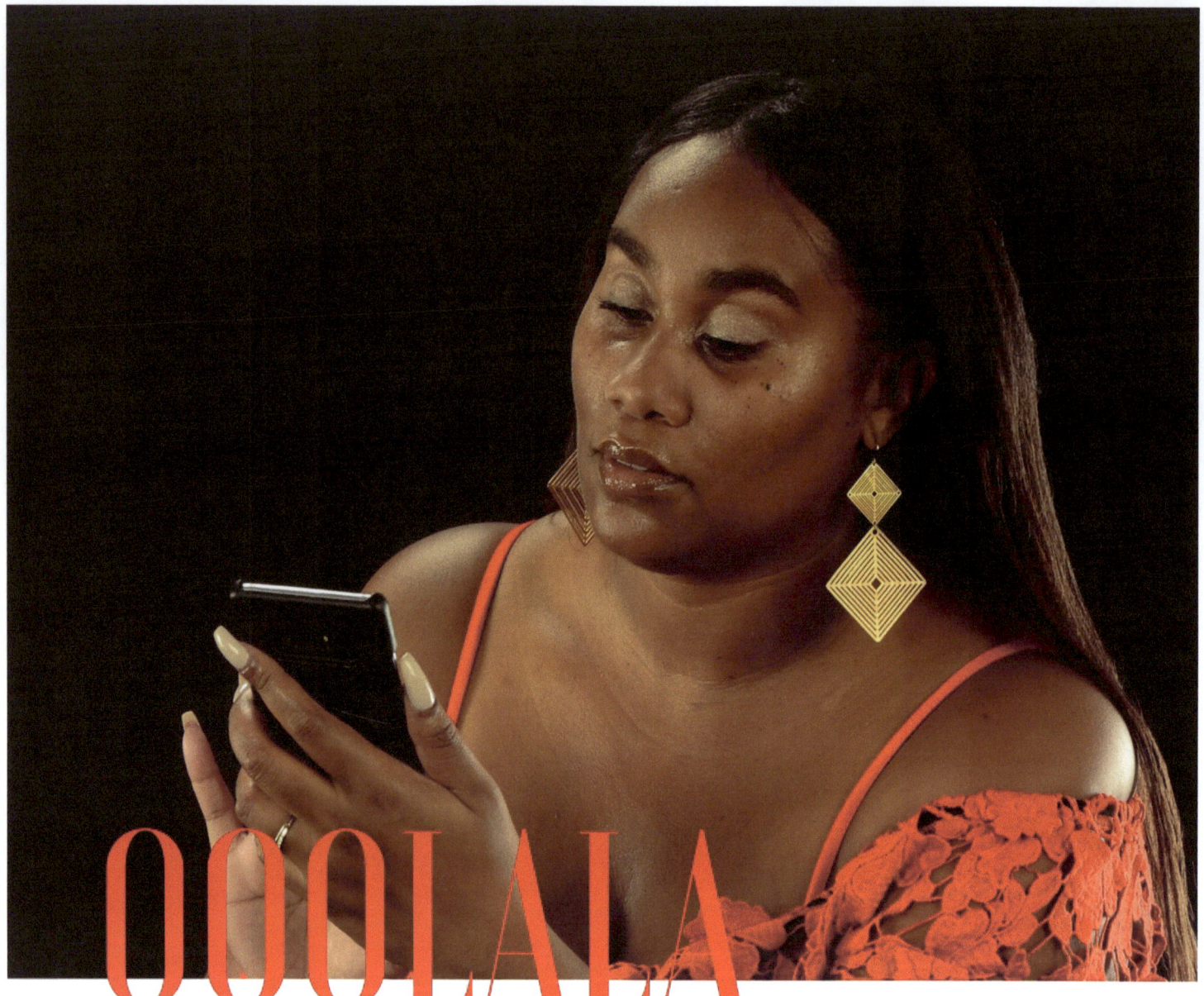

OooLaLa

THE BLOG TAKING OVER THE INTERNET

OooLaLaBlog.com
Instagram, Facebook and Twitter:
@OooLaLaBlog
YouTube channel: OooLaLa BlogPersonal
Instagram: @officialnjlala

Lanette Espy a.k.a "La La" is an award-winning journalist, blogger and media personality. In 2011, Lanette created her very own entertainment platform, OooLaLaBlog.com, and she built her own social media following of more than 200K. This New Jersey native has been featured on TMZ Live!, WBGO 88.3 FM, Hot 98.1 FM, and more. Throughout her journalism and blogging career, Lanette has interviewed many celebrities, reality stars, athletes and politicians, and she has covered all sorts of events, from the BET Experience in Los Angeles to Nas' listening party in Queens, NY. This blogger extraordinaire recently locked down a full-time gig as a digital producer, and in the future, she looks forward to publishing her first book.

"HOW CAN I STAND OUT FROM THE CROWD?".

fall /2019

Tips on being a successful blogger

with Lanette Espy a.k.a "La La"

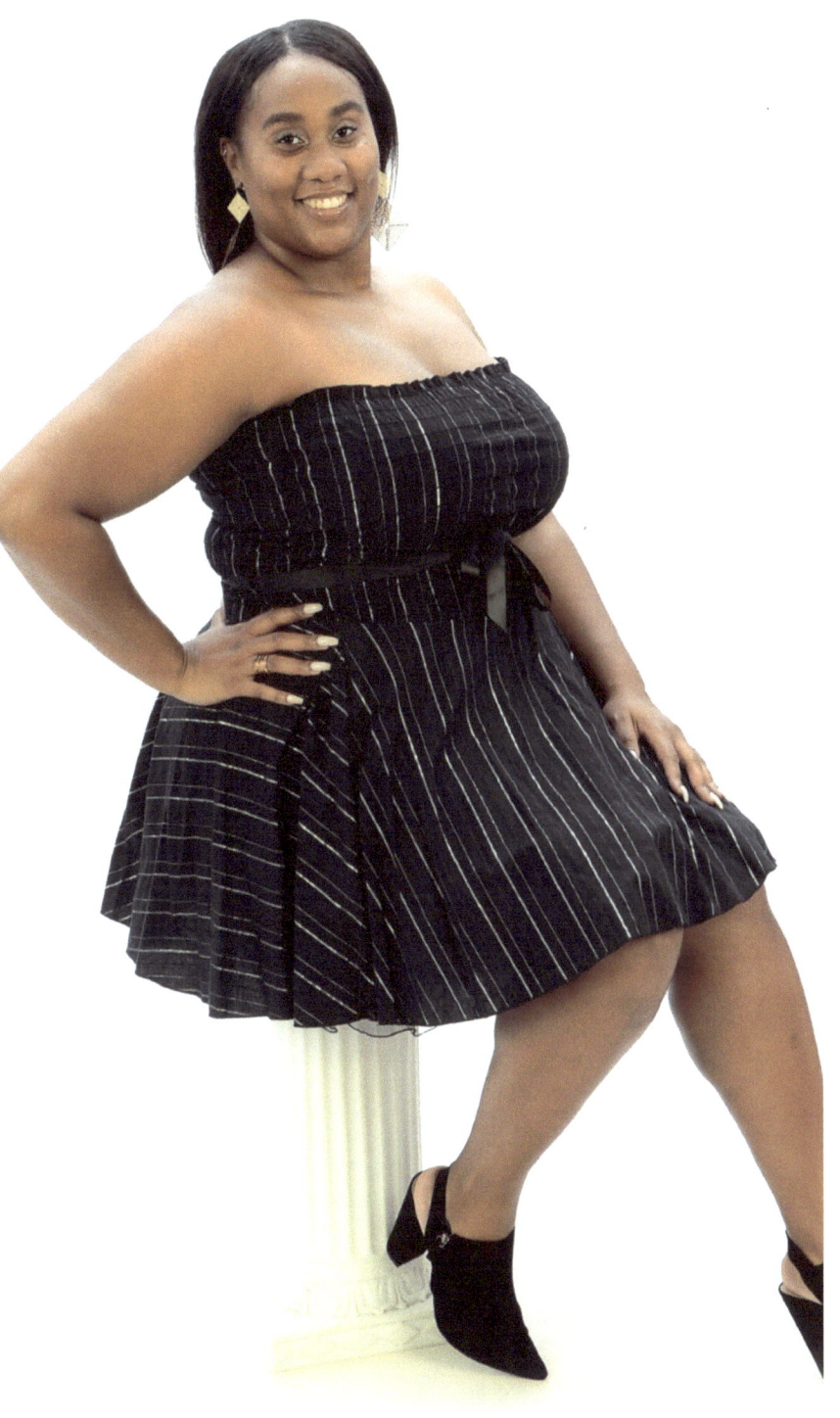

1) There are hundreds of celebrity gossip bloggers, travel bloggers, mommy bloggers, fashion bloggers, etc. But, never let that stop you from sharing your blogging gift with the world. Once establishing your specific niche, ask yourself: "how can I stand out from the crowd? What do I have to bring that's different and why would people be interested in what I have to say?" You have to add value to what you publish and create your own unique voice so you can build up a loyal following. Create a new series, new topics, and add some originality to your content. Also, make your blog stand out with branding. Pick and use the same color scheme, template design, font, logo, and use it consistently so when readers see your posts being shared, they know where it originally came from.

2) This connects with my first point in ways to stand out ... don't be afraid to voice your opinion and show your personality. Readers/followers love knowing a little about the face behind the blog so they have someone to connect with. Be authentic, be you and have fun with it!

3) Network, network, NETWORK! It's super important to collaborate with other people in your field. Network with other bloggers, PR people, celebrities, podcasters, YouTuber's, etc. Reach out to fellow bloggers online and don't be afraid to ask if you could write a guest post on their website. Writing guest posts on other blogs is smart because usually you can leave a link back to your own website which will not only help you gain exposure but will bring some traffic back to your own blog. Don't forget to "like," comment and share other people's content as well. Social media is all about engaging, so you also have to show your followers some love. You get further in this industry when you team up, help, learn and promote one another. Attend different industry events, get your face and your brand out there, and bring business cards so people remember you! And, don't forget to actually reach out to the people you meet at these events. Email them and link up online. Trust me, that goes a long way when it comes to building connections.

4) Don't just rely on social media to grow and maintain your blog. Although you should secure your blog name on all social media sites, social media shouldn't be the only thing you rely on when it comes to growing your following. I always say this, but we don't own our content on Instagram, Twitter, Facebook, etc. All bloggers should have their own website and email newsletter. Start growing your email list right away and secure your .com URL. Social media is a great addition to grow your fanbase and make money. But, if social media were to vanish today, where else would your followers find you? Where else could you make blog money? Always make sure you have a place where you own your content. And, don't just stop there. Venture out into creating and selling your own products, merch, blogging classes, e-books, etc. The possibilities are endless when it comes to expanding your brand and making money from it.

5) Soak in everything you can about the industry. Attend seminars, take an online social media or audience engagement course to brush up on your skills, learn from people who have been in the industry for years, and stay on top of new social media sites and trends. LinkedIn offers a variety of social media courses, codecademy.com offers free coding classes, melyssagriffin.com gives out awesome entrepreneur and blog tips, and take advantage of free business classes that may be offered at local community centers and libraries. There's so much to learn out there! Your brand is your baby and it's on you to nurture it and make it flourish. And, last but not least, don't forget to help out other newbies. Remember, we've all been there before. It doesn't hurt to pass along tips and advice. If you need to ask me a question, I'm only a DM away. And yes, I actually read and respond to my DM's.

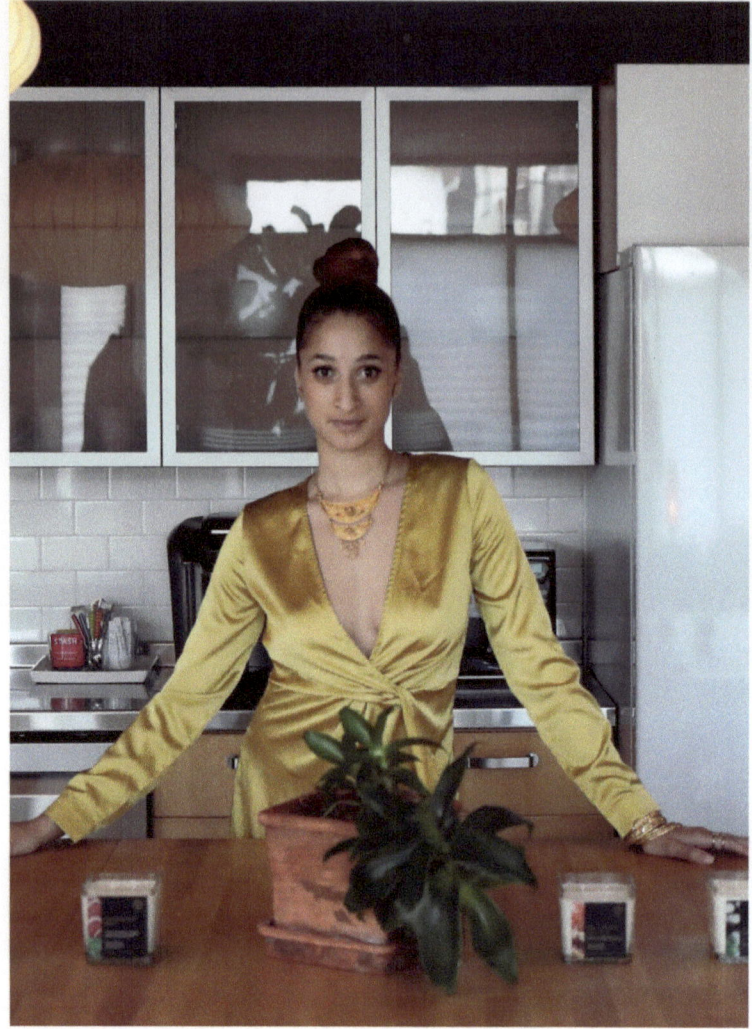
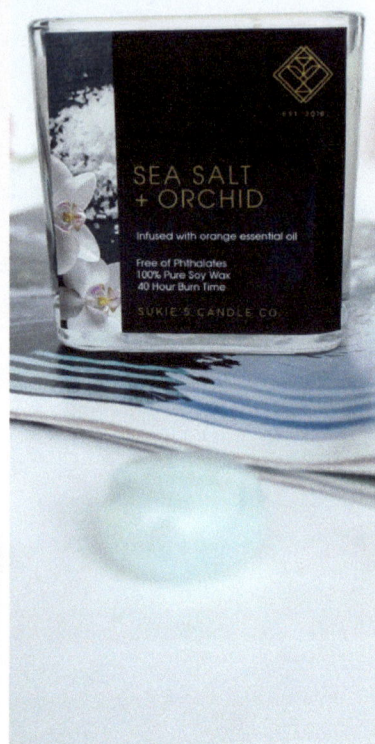

Sukies Candle Co

---

sukiescandleco.com

Unique & Rare AromasWe take pride in sourcing rare and memorable scents. Our collections are uniquely distinguished and exotically crafted, yielding an eco-friendly 40+ hour burn time.

Non-Toxic, Vegan, Eco-FriendlyOur candles have been mindfully sourced using 100% pure soy wax, derived domestically from American farmers. We always use lead & zinc free cotton wicks with phthalate-free fragrances. Infused with natural essential oils, each candle is petroleum-free and individually hand-poured in re-usable glass containers.

detailed information following answers to general Energy & Mood ShiftingWe believe in the power of candles to subtly shift our environments, thereby shifting consciousness. Our candles are an invitation to create soft atmospheric environments that promote peace, sensuality, & deep relaxation. We invite you to get lost in the sultry, intoxicating and exotically rich aromas. Cast spells of love, protection and bliss. Find the divine in the simple. From our hearts to yours, we sacredly pour these high intentions in to each of our candles.

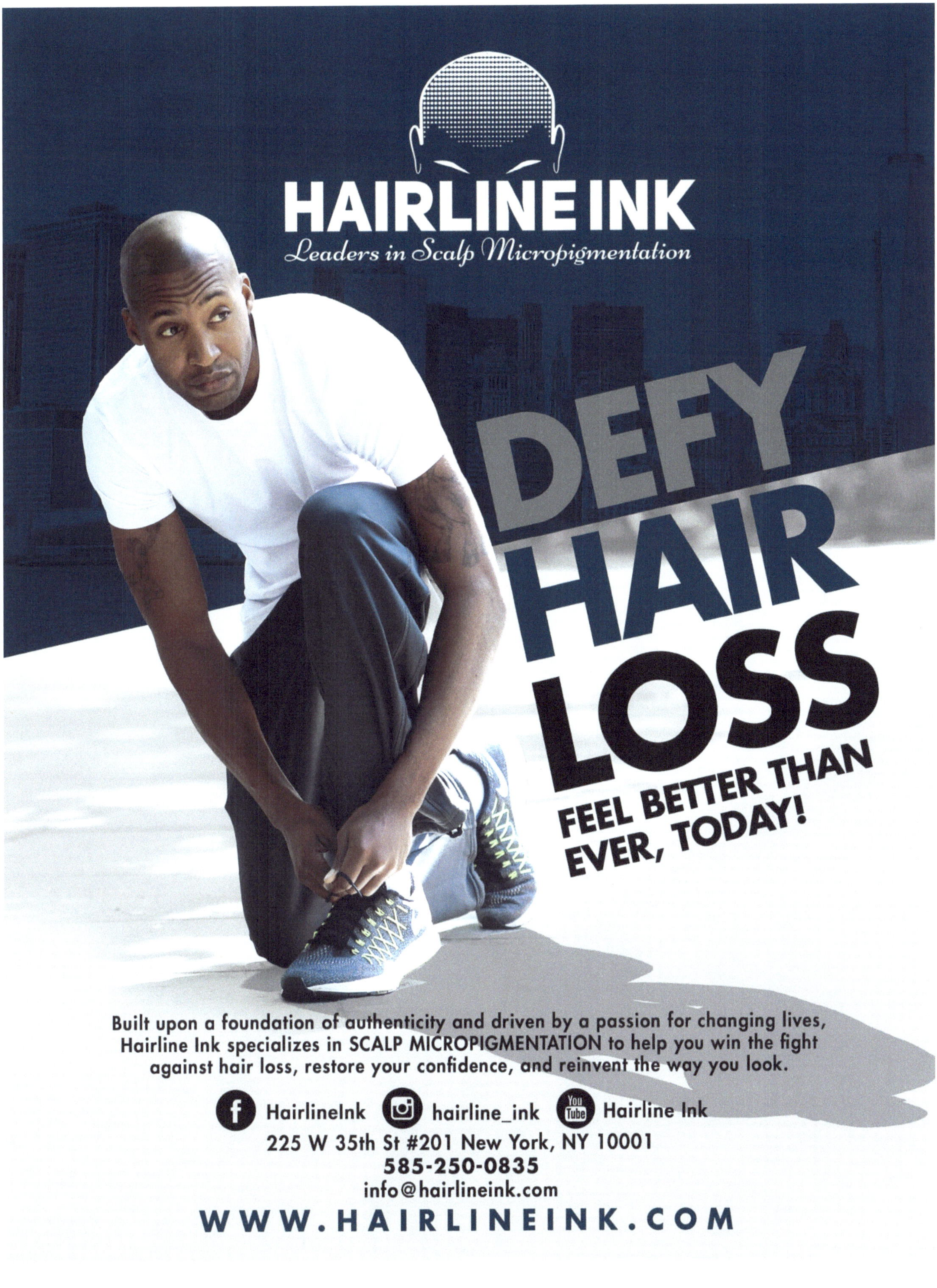

HAIRLINE INK
Leaders in Scalp Micropigmentation

DEFY HAIR LOSS
FEEL BETTER THAN EVER, TODAY!

Built upon a foundation of authenticity and driven by a passion for changing lives, Hairline Ink specializes in SCALP MICROPIGMENTATION to help you win the fight against hair loss, restore your confidence, and reinvent the way you look.

 HairlineInk   hairline_ink   Hairline Ink

225 W 35th St #201 New York, NY 10001
585-250-0835
info@hairlineink.com

WWW.HAIRLINEINK.COM

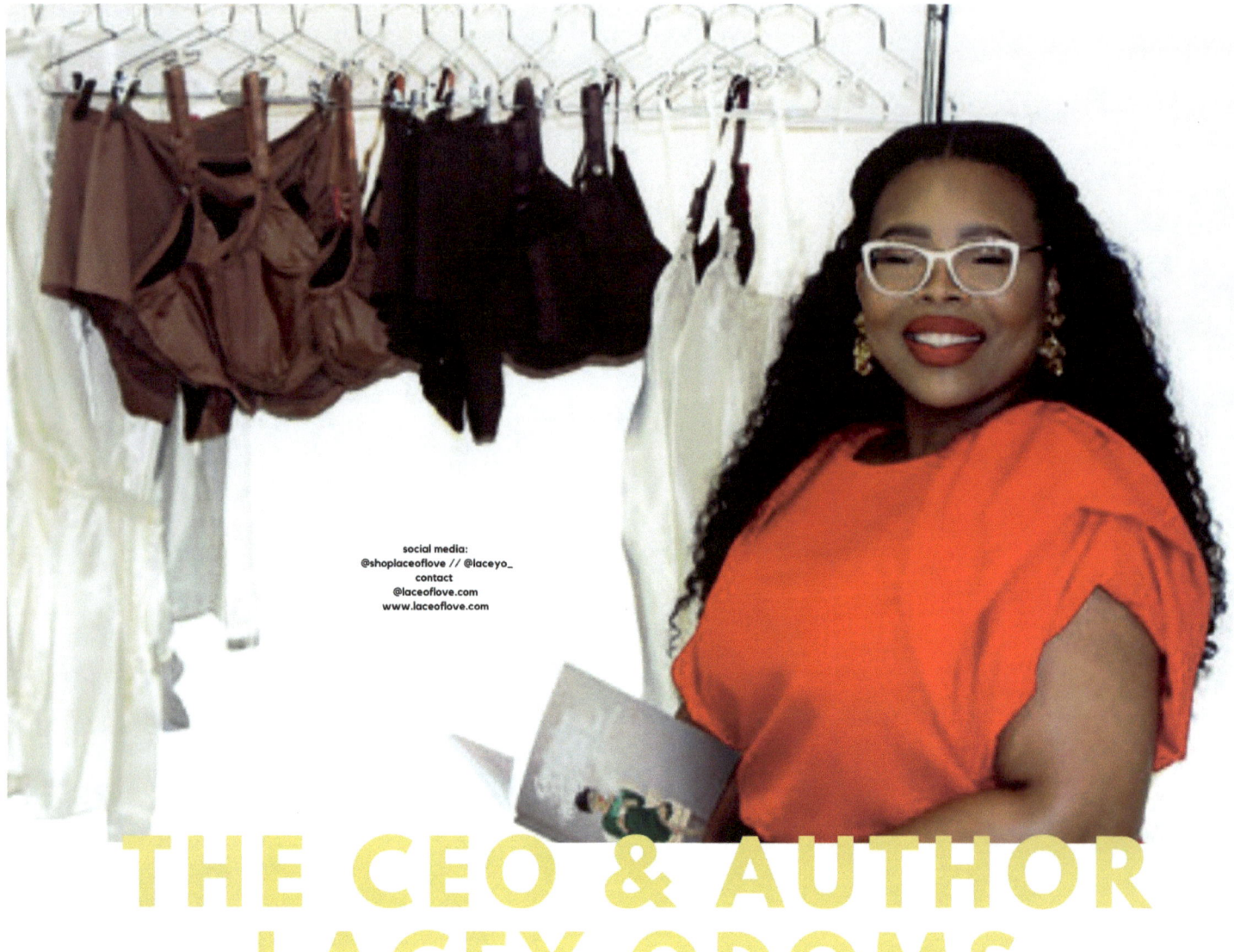

social media:
@shoplaceoflove // @laceyo_
contact
@laceoflove.com
www.laceoflove.com

THE CEO & AUTHOR LACEY ODOMS

This week we at Fashion Gxd Magazine sat down with Lacey Odoms. Lacey Odoms is an author and CEO of Lace of Love. After years of helping family and friends with large breast find fashionable and adequate, supportive bras, she decided to open Lace of Love. Lace of Love specializes in full-figured and plus-size lingerie with bra sizes starting at 28D to 54O. Lacey is a certified Bra Fitter and schedules her fittings on the weekends. Living proof, an entrepreneur can joggle a full-time job, run and operate a small business venture while squeezing in time to write and self-publish a poetry book, Conversations with the Heart and Soul. With over a decade of writing poetry for speaking events and as a freelance poetry writer, Ms. Odoms has a unique powerful voice that sheds light on everyday encounters in her newest collection of poems, Conversations with the Heart and Soul. This collection of poems centers around love, faith, hope, social issues, and being human. Much of her writing is heavily influenced by New Orleans' culture, issues experienced by individuals around the world, and her faith in Jesus Christ. Take a look at our exclusive interview with the rising brand.

Fashion Gxd Magazine: How did the idea for your business come about?

Answer: My business is two fold. I am both an author of a poetry book Conversations with the Heart and Soul and an online boutique owner of Lace of Love. I never really thought of writing a poetry book until a few years ago maybe in 2006 my pastor Tracy Cabsy Sr. stated I had books in me and my writing was going to take me places. After getting rejected so many times, through poetry journals, magazines, etc. my pastor words came back to me and I decided to gather up all the poems I ever wrote and find at least 60 of the best to put in a book. Originally, the book was title The Heart Speaks. I later changed the name to Conversations with the Heart and Soul to reflect these deep conversations . I would have with God on the matters of the heart which centered around life. The lingerie business started out of my need to find bras to fit my large breast and small back and my desire to help other females find their right bra size. After years of helping family and friends with large breast find fashionable, comfortable and supportive bras, I decided to open Lace of Love. Lace of Love specializes in full-figured and plus-size lingerie with bra sizes starting at 28D to 54O.

Fashion Gxd Magazine: How do you find people to bring into your organization that truly care about the organization the way you do?

Answer: Currently, I take on the multitude of responsibilities for the business by myself and with the help of my close family. When I am working my normal 9 to 5, they package orders or respond to inquires, etc. They have truly been a blessing to me and my company

Fashion Gxd Magazine: What three pieces of advice would you give to other children who want to become entrepreneurs?

Answer: 1. Seek God to discover if what you desire to do lines up with His purpose for your life. 2. If it does, find a mentor who can pour into you that has a business in that same industry you desire to establish a business. 3. The most important skill is to learn. Study and gain knowledge by reading, researching and taking courses or going to seminars either online or face to face that involves running a successful business, marketing, and negotiating, networking and sharpening your skill set in the industry you will start a company within. Never stop learning.

Fashion Gxd Magazine: If you had the chance to start your career over again, what would you do differently?

Answer: I would have worked harder to find a mentor in my field. I believe it's critical to have a mentor to properly guide and direct you. God covered me with His grace until He blessed me with a good mentor. My mentor guidance saved me time and money. Their level of expertise isn't rooted in a book or YouTube video.

Fashion Gxd Magazine: What would you say are the top three skills needed to be a successful entrepreneur

Answer: 1. Communication is the blood of the company. If you do not listen to what the customers want or what the employees need, your business will fail 2. You must be creative and willing to think outside of the box to keep an advantage over the competition. Constantly, challenge yourself to be creative and come up with creative ideas. Take time everyday to write the ideas down. 3. You must be flexible. The blueprint you created for your business, or that marketing plan may not go as planned. When things do not go as you intended, don't panic, get creative and pray. God will see you through. If you allow yourself to be flexible, challenges will not overtake you but will make you stronger and wiser to overcome the challenges.Fashion Gxd Magazine: What have been some of your failures, and what have you learned from them?

Answer: I am a firm believer, failure is our greatest teacher, so a lot of things I learned could have only been learned through my trails. I appreciate the hard life lessons because it made me a stronger and wiser person. But most importantly, the challenges and trails of life and business helped to equip me for elevation.

Fashion Gxd Magazine: How many hours do you work a day on average?
Answer: I would say about 4 to 5 hrs a day or more when needed for my personal business.

Fashion Gxd Magazine: Describe/outline your typical day?

Answer: Currently, I have a normal 9 to 5. I work out of state and it requires an hour and twenty minutes commute going and sometimes coming back it may take 2 hours depending on the traffic. On most mornings, I am up at 5am to start my day. Some mornings I may get up at 4:30am or a littler earlier to get a jump start on talking to vendors out of the country. On my breaks at work, I will respond to emails, schedule appointments, order supplies, inventory, etc. for my company and when I get home I continue working for my company taking care of anything that is needed such as packaging orders, etc. which can go until 12am or a little later in the morning. Also, I may have a bra fitting scheduled between 5:30pm and 7pm directly when I get off the 9 to 5. I will soon be scheduling bra fittings only on every other Friday and Saturday to help better manage my time to take on other projects.

Fashion Gxd Magazine: How has being an entrepreneur affected your family life?

Answer: I come from a family of entrepreneurs. My parents and brother have their own trucking company, so growing up with entrepreneurs I have become accustomed to adjusting my schedule when needed to conduct business, cook dinner or engage in family time. Date night with my King is always scheduled every other Friday out of the month. I also make sure my mother and I have Saturday girl's day at least once a month and

FGM | October 2019

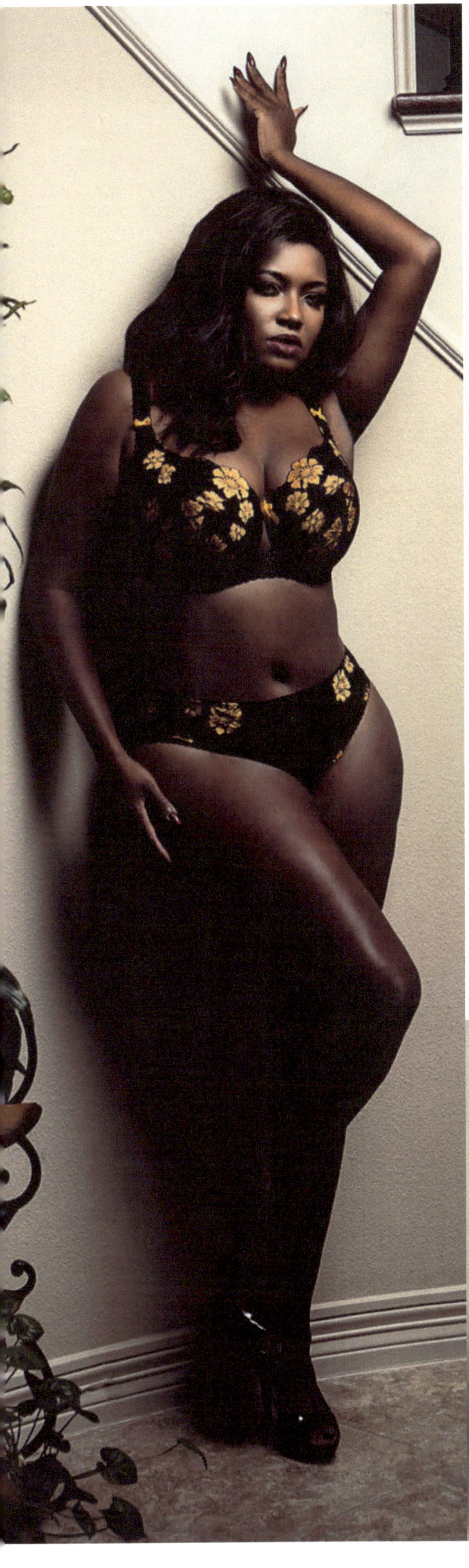

Author and CEO of Lace of Love

family dinner with both of my parents at least once a week. My family is very important to me so I ensure I make time to spend with my family.

Fashion Gxd Magazine: What motivates you?

Answer: There are many things and people that motivates me. Seeing other entrepreneurs especially females and young blacks working hard building successful companies lets me know it's possible for me to be just as successful. In addition, my family, friends and pastor motivates me to continue to press in the face of adversity while keeping God first. Writing also helps to motivate me to continue to strive to complete my God ordained purpose here on earth. Myles Monroe gave a sermon and he talked about using the gifts God gave you. My desire is to die empty to where the gifts and talents God placed in me has been used up completely when I leave this earth.

Fashion Gxd Magazine: How do you generate new ideas?

Answer: Mainly, I generate new ideas by spending time with myself and God. In addition, I may write or sketch if I have a certain vision in my head, reading, listening to interviews or looking at bodies of works of those I admire.

Fashion Gxd Magazine: What sacrifices have you had to make to be a successful entrepreneur?

Answer: I have sacrificed a lot of time in working toward completing deadlines so I could not always enjoy spending time with my loved ones. Time is one of those commodities you can never get back but the return can be great. I try to use my time wisely and things I may desire to do I don't because it may not be an efficient use of my time.

Fashion Gxd Magazine : Where you see yourself and your business in 10 years? 20 years?

Answer: In 10 years, I pray that I have a physical boutique and manufacturing products under my company brand. In addition, I will continue to write poetry books or any genre God leads me to write that will inspire and help others while traveling the world pouring into others through speaking events. 20 years from now I see myself continuing to build Lace of Love expanding it into clothing and beauty products for the family and build my personal brand as an author and speaker. My goal is to establish a household brand that inspires, motivates and encourages individuals through fashion and words.You can find Ms. Odoms poetry book Conversations with the Heart and Soul and her lingerie boutique online at www.laceoflove.com . In addition, Conversations with the Heart and Soul can be purchased on Amazon (www.amazon.com) , (www.barnesandnobel.com) and www.volopressbooks.com.For inquiries regarding freelance poetry writing, speaking engagements or services related to Ms. Odoms lingerie business, feel free to contact her at contact@laceoflove.com.

Bottom Model: Shawn Reaves @hourglass_corsetiere | Hair and Makeup: Shawn Reaves Lingerie: Beautiful Black and Gold bra and panties inspired by Nola Saints @shoplaceoflove Lace of Love www.laceoflove.com | Location: Mgriffin Studios, Cypress Texas | Photographer: Morris Griffin | Photographer: Jewel Tolson Kozak Asst. to Photographer: Anita Griffin / Top Model: Roxy Perez @poproxx428 | Hair and Makeup: Roxy Perez| Lingerie: Sexy Teal with Black Lace Chemise @shoplaceoflove Lace of Love www.laceoflove.com Location: Mgriffin Studios, Cypress Texas | Photographer: Morris Griffin @moeman34Photographer: Jewel Tolson Kozak | Asst. to Photographer: Anita Griffin

Picture of Owner Lacey Odoms | Stylist: Lacey Odoms @laceyo_ | Photographer: Tyesha Scott @angless___ | MUA: Mia Paternostro @facesbymiasimone | Hair Stylist: Dana Winfield @hairbydanaw | Hair Extensions: Seven Zen Hair @sevenzenhair | Book: Conversations with the Heart and Soul @shoplaceoflove www.laceoflove.com/book

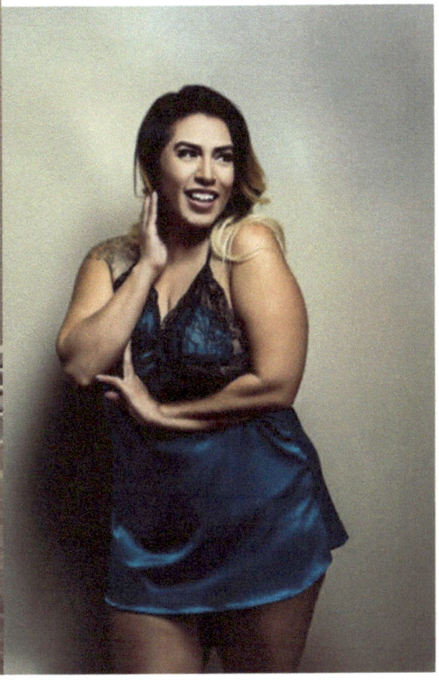

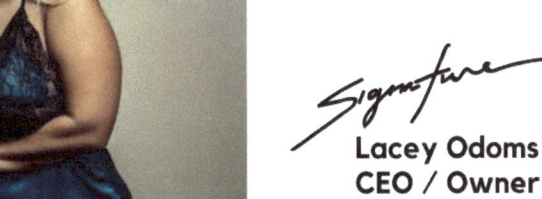

Lacey Odoms
CEO / Owner

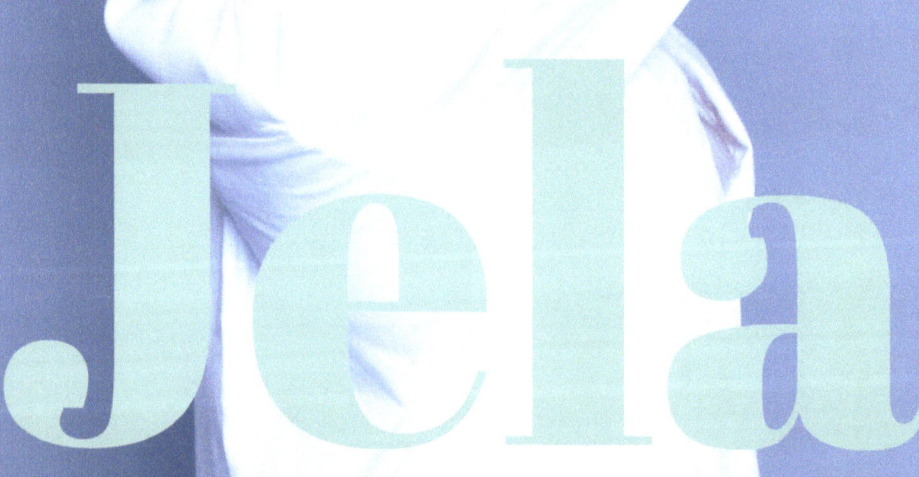

COVER STORY

Jela
THE ED
S

WRITTEN BY: NOVIA ROSE @NOVEEROSE

Written By: Novia Rose @noveerose

THE LAST OF THE BAD GIRLS

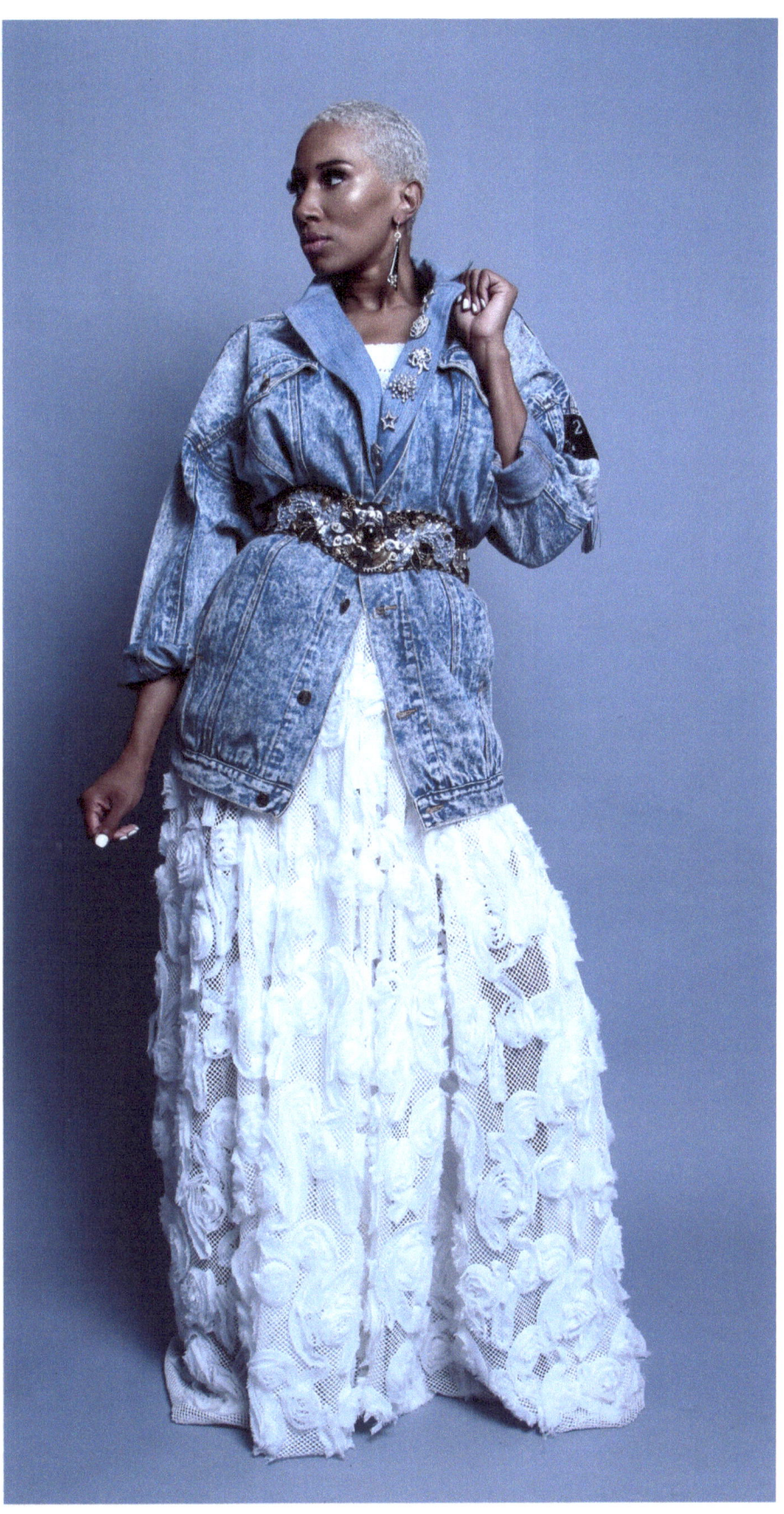

Life after The Bad Girls Club has not been too shabby for Alum, Jela Lanier! While traveling and landing several modeling opportunities, Jela is also creating her footing in the fashion industry with several projects and distinct goals.

"Life has been very interesting for me, coming off of reality TV, you have to figure out your niche and how readjust to living a "regular" life. So that is what life has really been about for me, just finding the balance of Jela, the persona, Jelaminah the Entrepreneur, the career woman, the model, actress, & figuring out how to do it all at once."

Being completely transparent, the former BGC star explains how Reality TV affects her everyday life:

"In my career, because I pride myself on being very educated, very well spoken, I think that a lot of the times Reality TV gives people a bad rap. I think that people judge you because you've been on a reality show and they already have a preconceived notion about who you are and who you aren't. I am constantly fighting that stereotype.

Jela explained how she finds the perfect balance between modeling and other areas of her career:

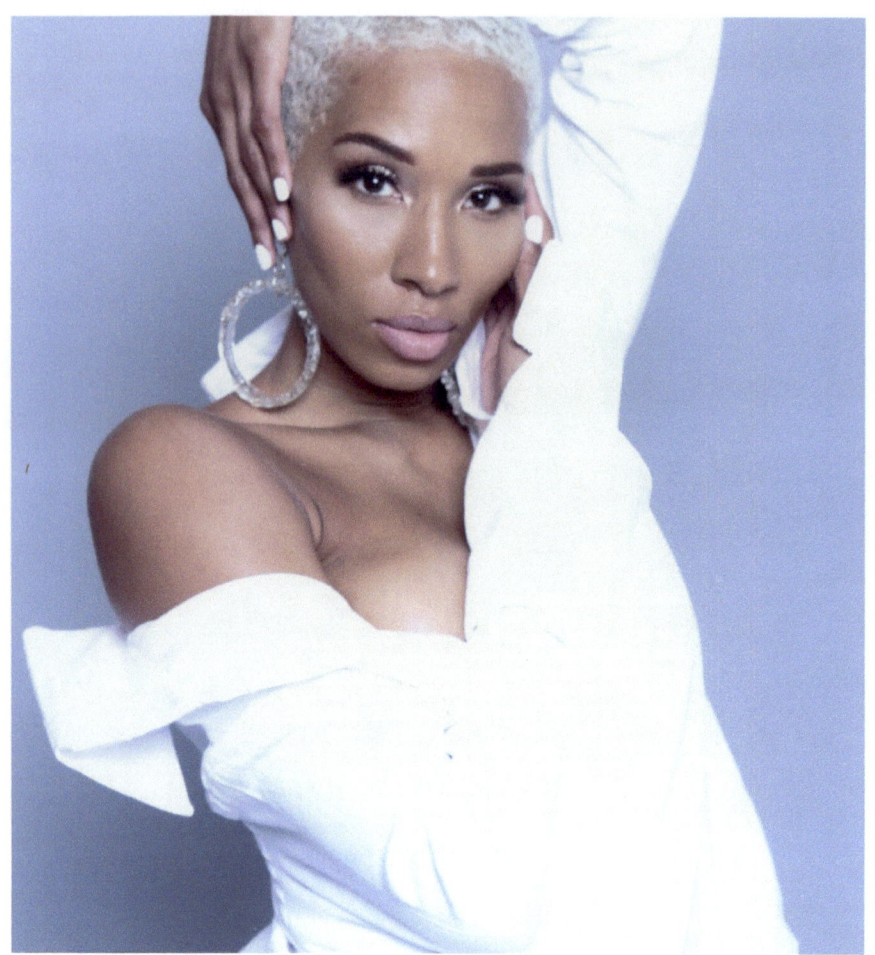
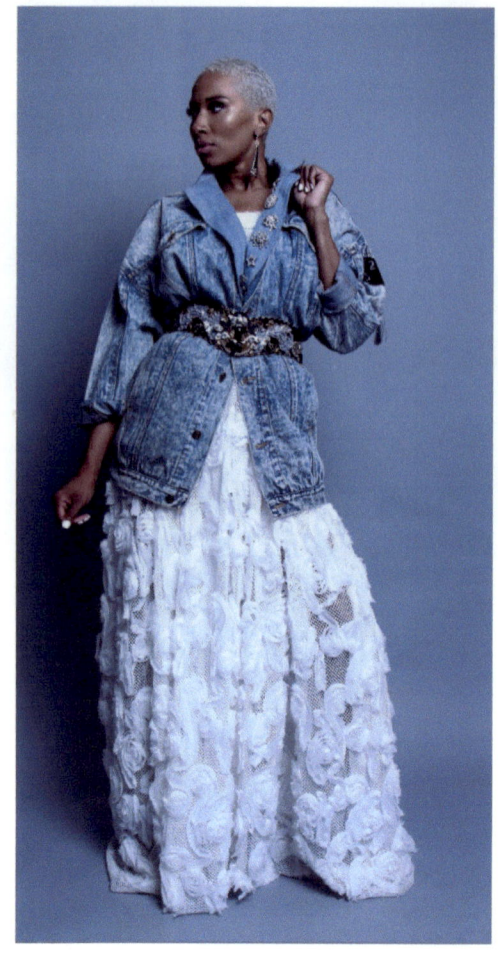

"Right now is the time of year that I am dedicating to my modeling career. So I may take 3 to 6 months out of the year and solely dedicate that to nothing but pushing my modeling career, and pushing my clothing line. Nothing else takes precedence over that. I got picked up to do Paris Fashion week in March 2020. So I'll be walking in the Spring, but right now I am actually going to Paris to network and see agencies. Really just be around everyone else, other models and designers."

Though Jela recently started her clothing line, Normal Culture, she also reveals that every model faces the time where they have to choose between designing or walking. For her, modeling isn't an option:

"Modeling for sure. I have been passionate about that and being in front of a camera since I was a child and the clothing line is something I started after I left BGC just to give my fans something to stay connected to me. I eventually grew a love for it, but I never saw myself being

a fashion designer, never saw myself drawing up a clothing line, never."

JELA

COVER STORY

Crediting Rihanna as her biggest inspiration, Jela is setting her sights on a bright future that includes breaking into the acting roles, nabbing a great contract with a top modeling agency, and a high end endorsement deal.

Jela's go-to fashion items are Converses, cute white high-waisted jeans, a good pair of boyfriend jeans and short sexy dresses. Essentially, items that can be dressed up or down. Her top five high end brands are Louis Vuitton, Fenty, Chanel, YSL, and Prada. Everyday brands, Zara, Top Shop, Free People, BCBG, Gray Scale (@fromgrayscale), and Hanifa (@HanifaOfficial)

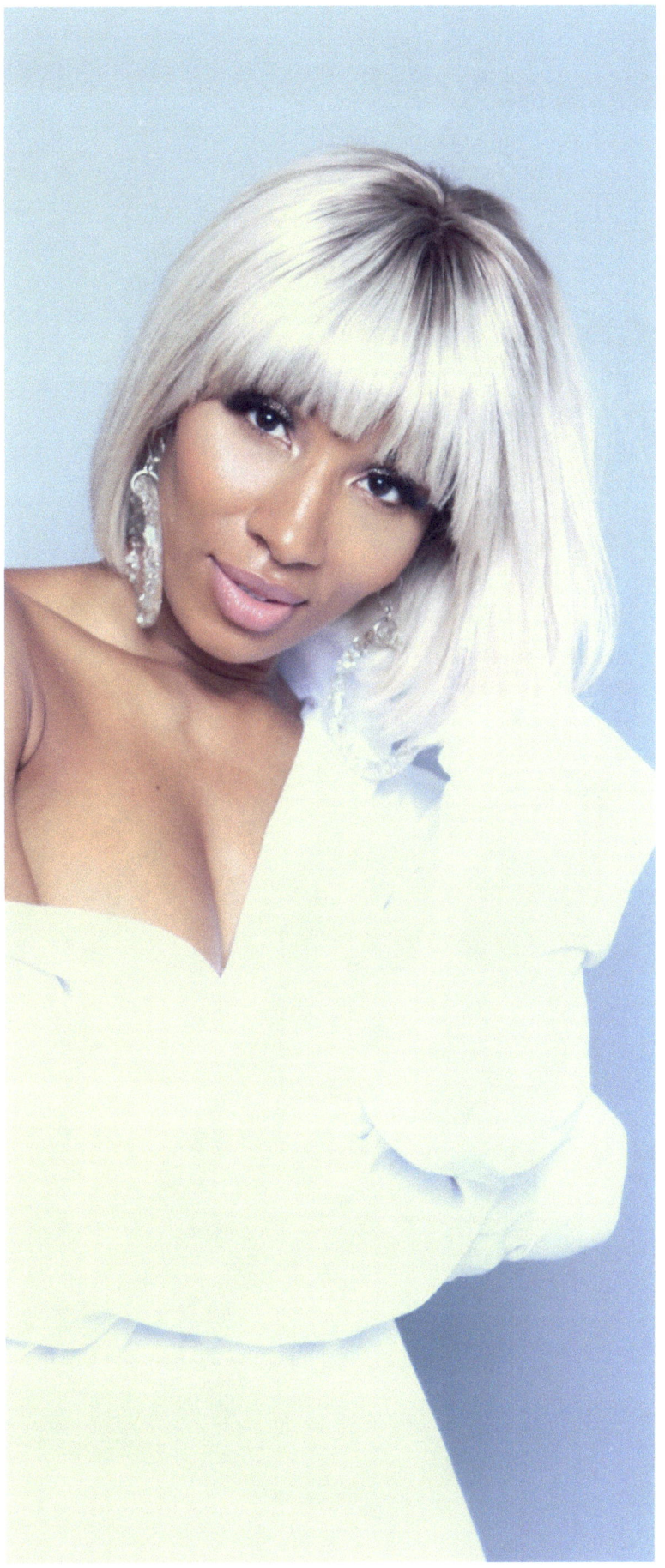

THE POWER OF Quincy Chad

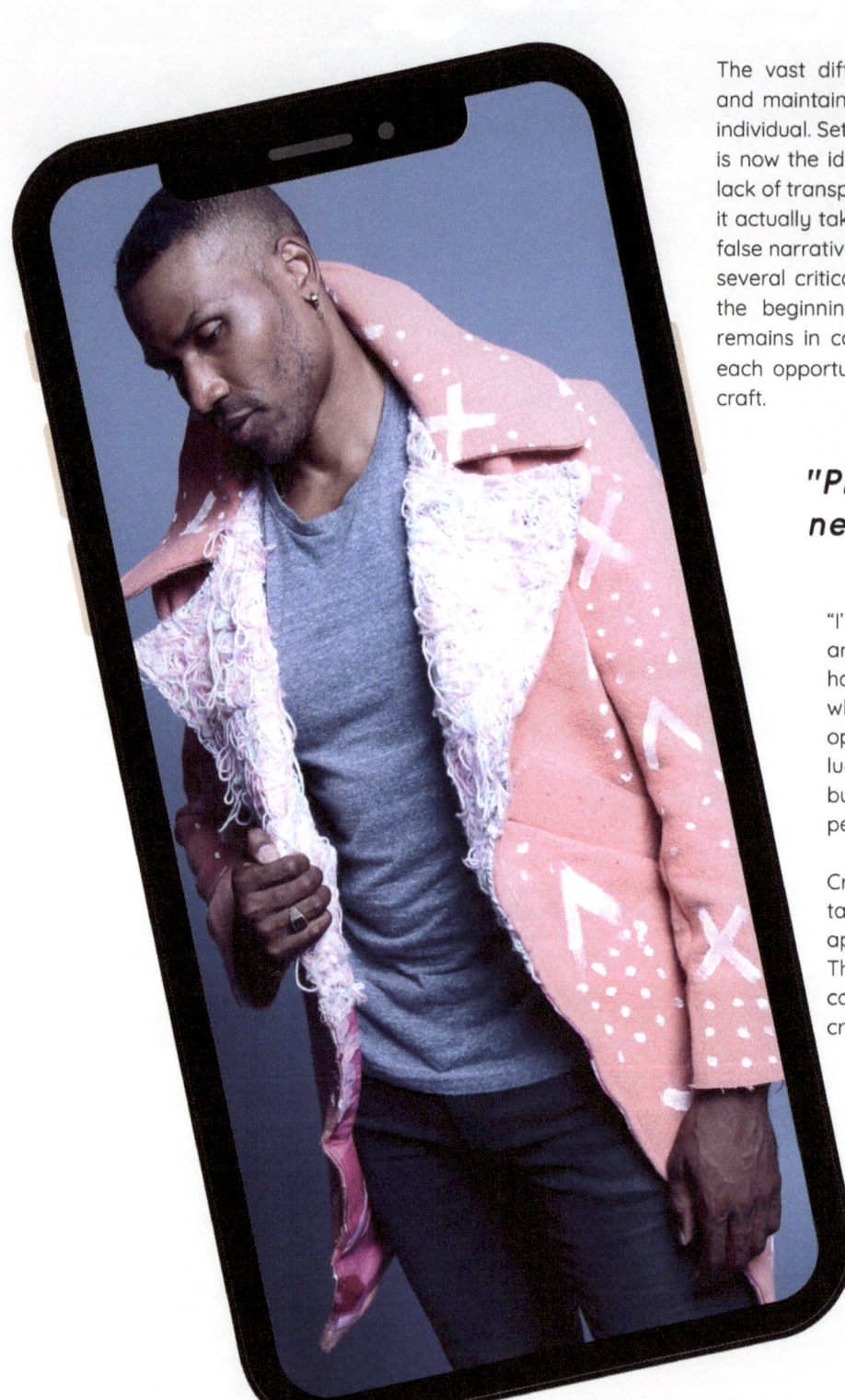

The vast difference between attaining success quickly and maintaining successful is the determination of each individual. Setting goals that are beyond any expectations is now the ideal mantra of this generation. However the lack of transparency, in addition to social media and what it actually takes to accomplish these goals, often creates false narratives. Quincy Chad has already landed roles on several critically acclaimed shows. Although he is still in the beginning stages of his career, the rising Actor remains in constant preparation mode, is motivated by each opportunity, and has a deep understanding of his craft.

"Plenty of talented people never get the chance."

"I'm very lucky. I've met a ton of Actors that are amazingly talented, and even they haven't had the opportunities that I've had. It's kind of where preparation meets LUCK, and that's opportunity. Sometimes, you just gotta get lucky. Everybody works hard, especially in this business, but like I said, plenty of talented people never get the chance."

Crediting his Grandmother for discovering his talent at a young age, acting has always been apart of Chad's story. In addition to 'Orange Is The New Black', his latest role on 'POWER' comes as no surprise as he continues to create a presence on our TV Screens:

"It's Excellent! I'm having a lot of fun. Met a lot of interesting people, and you know the acting community, once you've been working for a little bit, it tends to get really small. You get on set and you may know someone in Production, a Production Assistant, a Writer from somewhere else, you know, so they welcomed me with open arms and it was a family atmosphere right from the jump." Though he did not give away the ultimate fate of "Zig",

FASHION GXD MAGAZINE

Preparation. Be present.

Quincy opened up about what kind of roles he feels will bring out the best of his abilities... "It's funny, because when I first started acting, I gravitated towards playing villains. I always wanted to play a villain. My favorite character of all time was when Heath Ledger played 'The Joker'. Also, Tom Hardy as Bane. Something about those characters just jumping into a totally different space, having a different voice, size, everything, it's a total shift in that person.

Unfortunately, Quincy can't reveal the current projects that he is working on, BUT that villain role eventually did come through. He previously starred in "Standing Eight", a film about a Boxer who develops Lupus. It is now available on Amazon Video. Chad also spoke on a significant part or technique of acting that is rarely mentioned: "A lot of people just see what happens when you're on set, then boom, the show comes out and that's it, so they think they can do it, but there's a lot of preparation involved, there's a lot of hard work and sweat, not sleeping, you know, people don't know that part. They just see when you book the gig and when it comes out. They don't know that you heard "no" a thousand times before that."

As for the future..... "Part of the game for me is just to take it day by day, obviously we have our goals. It's one of those things where you have to focus on the task at hand. If you're looking 2, 3, 4, 5 months ahead, you're not focused on exactly what you're doing right now. Like we talked about, preparation. Be present.

So for me, if you have caribbean parents you'll understand. My parents are from Trinidad, when you tell your parents you want to be an actor, they're like, "What the hell is that?". My dad is in finance and my mom is in the corporate world as well, so it is more so about structure. They worry about you, but I've always been a dreamer......."...

& clearly a hard worker! Be sure to look out for Quincy in all of his upcoming roles and future projects! Chad defines his signature style as an equal balance between comfort and remaining fashion forward, yet versatile. He lists sweats and always having something WHITE (preferably footwear) as his everyday must haves. Don't be fooled though, when it's time to suit up, he will most definitely deliver.

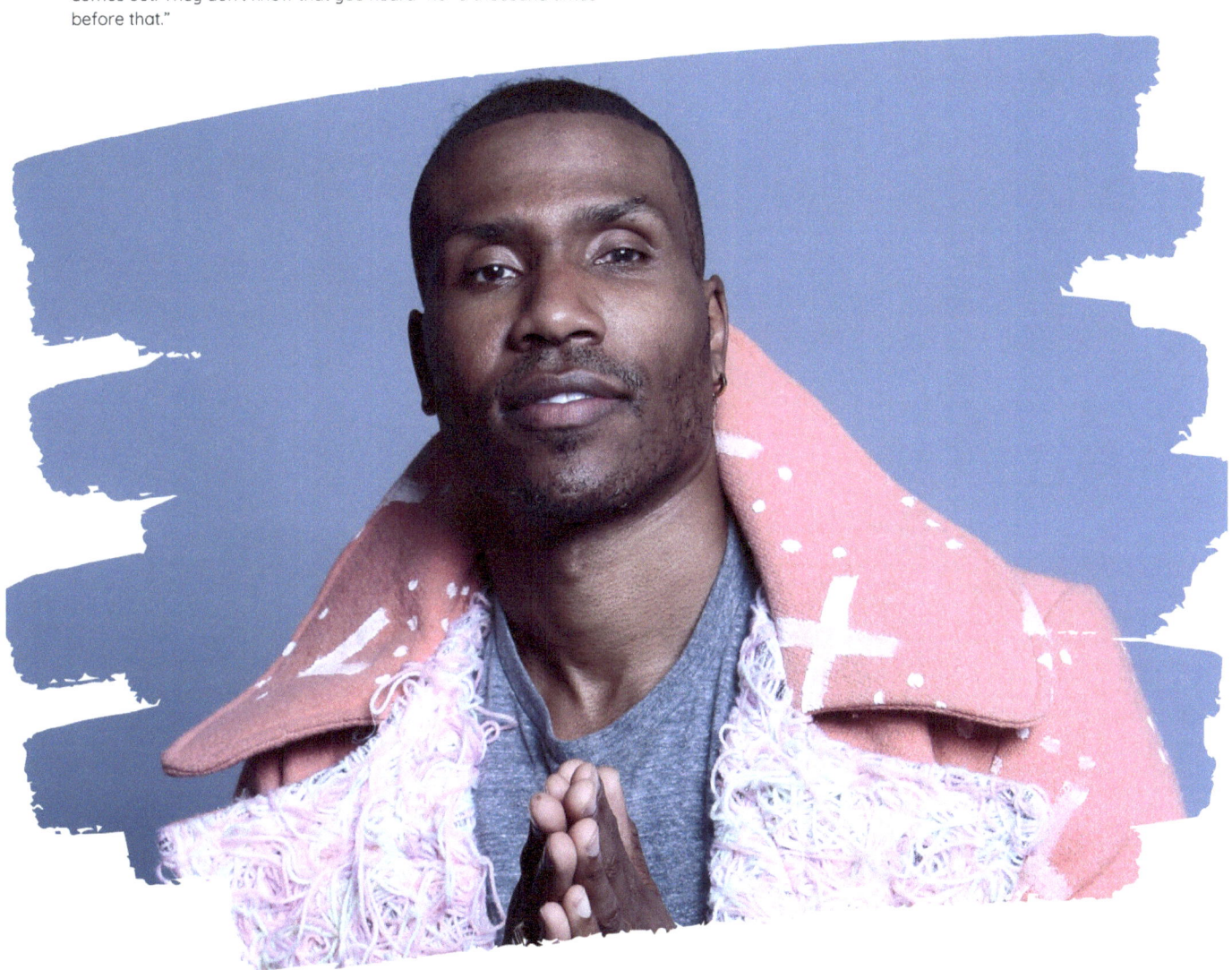

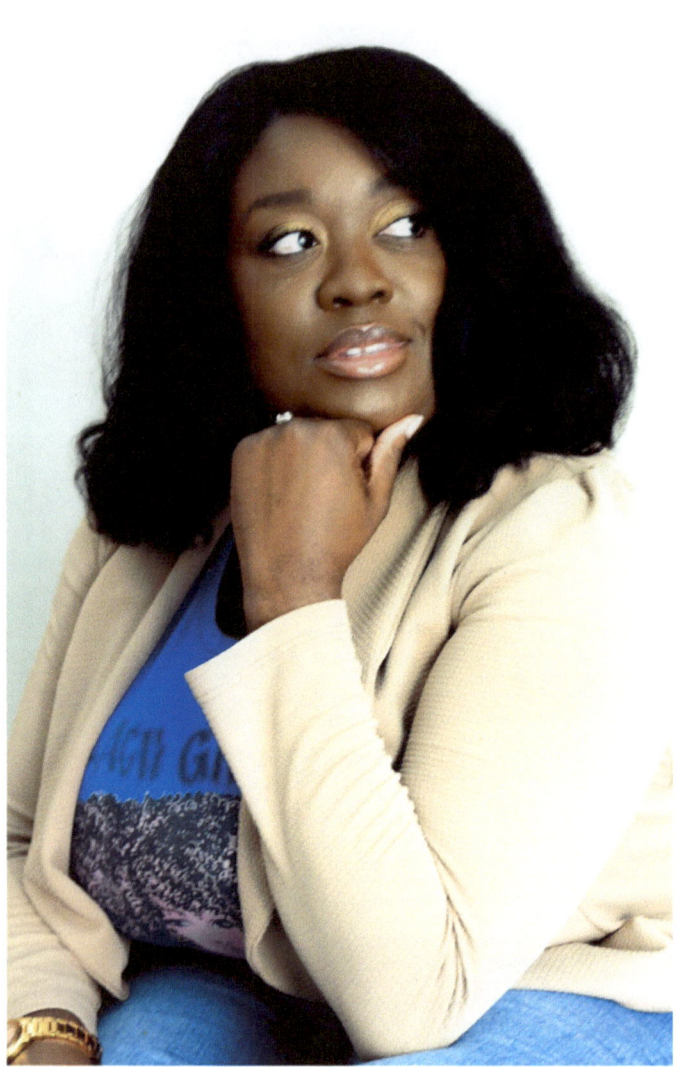
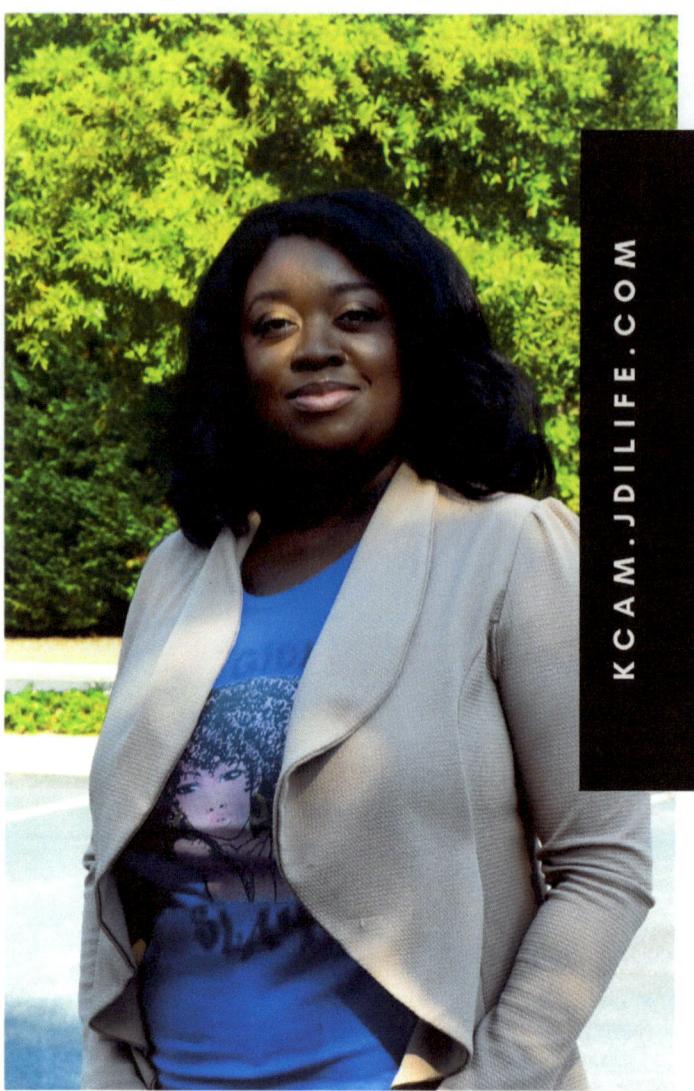

KCAM.JDILIFE.COM

ELEVATE YOURSELF WITH KRISTEN CAMERON

Kristen Cameron is an aspiring entrepreneur and Independent Distributor for JDI Life. The company specializes in providing natural supplements based on stem cell nutrition, which have been developed with proprietary formulas to help combat chronic pain and various health issues. During the day, she works at a background screening firm where she has several years of experience leading a team of compliance specialists. After learning what a particular product (Vita-Stim) had done for her sister diagnosed with Relapsing Remitting Multiple Sclerosis, she was intrigued by the technology behind the supplement. Compared to the expensive medications prescribed that brought along a host of side effects, the Vita-Stim pill kept the symptoms manageable and almost non-existent. Her sister wasn't the only success story. The physician who formulated the product used it himself to help treat an auto-immune disease which produced the same type of results.* These testimonials helped propel Kristen to try it herself and once she experienced her own results (eliminated hip pain following a car accident and increased energy), she recently decided to make it a personal mission to help those who are plagued with health concerns by becoming a Distributor and educating others about stem cell nutrition. Kristen and the JDI Life Team is dedicated to changing lives by meeting the market demand for a more natural way to build up their health internally. Her passion in life is helping others and is the driving force behind her current business pursuits. In her downtime, you will find her spending time with family and friends, enjoying a good movie or book, playing with hair and makeup, or looking for a beach to relax on with her husband. *Nothing in this message is to be construed as diagnosing, treating, preventing or curing any disease. No statements have been evaluated by the Food & Drug Administration

SOCIAL MEDIA HANDLE :
INSTAGRAM @JDILIFE18LINKEDIN
LINKEDIN.COM/IN/KRISTEN-CAMERON-218B4066
PHOTO CREDIT: TARA DUNCAN

BOLD KULTURE BEAUTY

BEN Y. HALLMARK

Kristal Cunningham is a wife, mother of two handsome young men, and a pharmacist who loves living life boldly. Fueled by her passion for beautiful curly hair, she began Bold Kulture Beauty after noticing a lack of access to quality products that met her curly hair needs. "I wanted to show people that hair care can be simple, knowing your hair coupled with the use of quality products is a recipe for hair care success!" – Kristal Cunningham founder of Bold Kulture Beauty

Kristal is dedicated to helping others embrace their natural beauty through the use of image positive minority developed hair care and beauty products. She believes that beauty begins with self-love and is manifested through confidence. Understanding the need for self-representation in beauty, her mission is to empower women to feel beautiful and be confident knowing that they have the tools to meet their beauty needs.

Bold Kulture Beauty was founded out of necessity, Bold Kulture Beauty is designed to show those with natural hair that hair care can be simple. Realizing how overwhelming the search for sound advice and high-quality products can be, Bold Kulture Beauty was designed to alleviate that stress and bringing both sound advice and high-quality products all under one roof! Using the skills she developed over 12 years as a clinical pharmacist, Kristal is able to dispel the myths and bring you the facts about hair care and why quality matters.

Visit BoldKulture.com for tips on stress-free hair care, advice on how to address natural hair care with a positivity first approach, education, live consultations, and hand-selected high quality products to meet your haircare and beauty needs.

Social Media Handles:
Facebook/ Pinterest: Bold Kulture Beauty**Instagram:** @boldkulturebeauty**Twitter:** @boldkulture**YouTube:** Bold Kulture Beauty

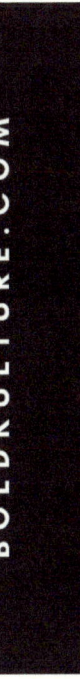
BOLDKULTURE.COM

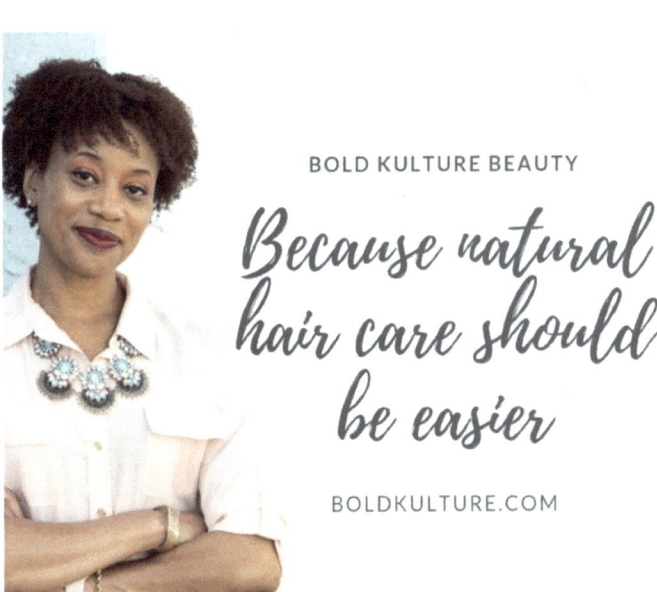

BOLD KULTURE BEAUTY

Because natural hair care should be easier

BOLDKULTURE.COM

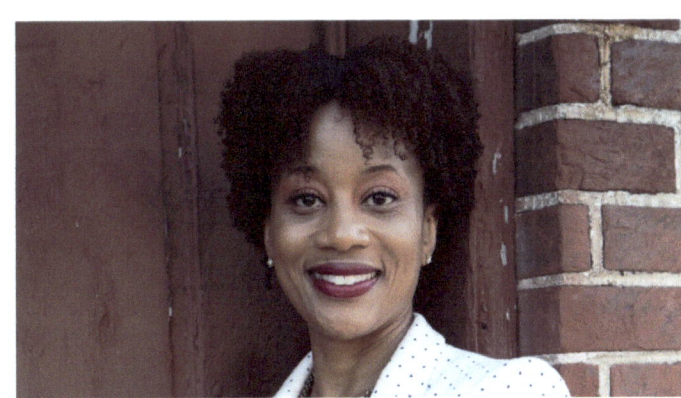

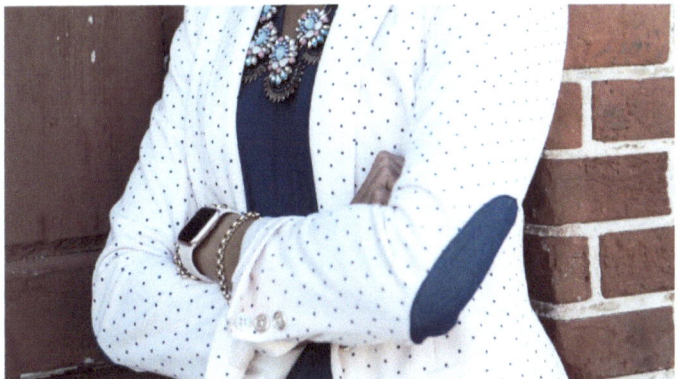

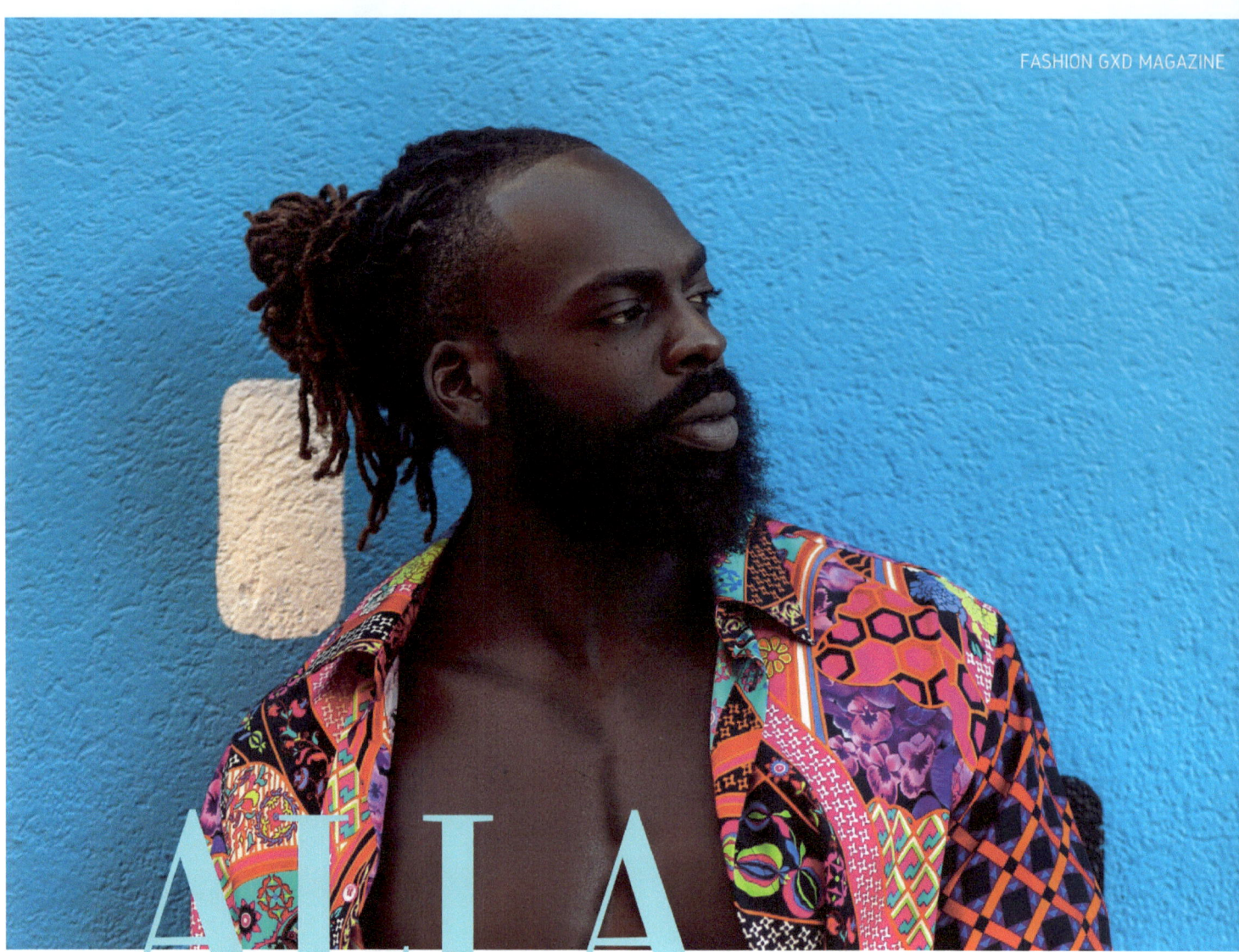

FASHION GXD MAGAZINE

ALI A
AFONJ

INTERVIEW BY:
VON BOOZIER TWINS

> I wanted to develop an opportunity for my family and be a role model for other Black male professionals.

Ali Afonja is on a mission to change the narrative and end the stigma and shame of mental health awareness while helping others to live their best lives. Through his company Family Restoration Services, Ali Afonja provides resources focused on helping parents that have children with emotional, cognitive, developmental, and behavioral disorders. The Von Boozier Twins caught up with Afronja as he shares his journey and mission to positively impact and inspire his community through therapeutic approaches.

Tell us a little about your brand and how you've come to this vastly successful peek in your career?

My practice, Family Restoration Services, provides mental health treatment using a holistic approach. We have developed a 4-quadrant approach to wellness which focuses on fitness, nutrition, spirituality and cognition. Our unique approach has contributed vastly to the company's success. Further, my devote commitment to a healthy lifestyle has led me into a sub career of physique competitions, modeling and consulting.

What inspired you to become an entrepreneur?

I did not observe many black mental health professionals as a youth and I have always been focused on wellness.

Tell us about a time when you showed determination to continue as an entrepreneur?

In 2009, when I began to focus on holistic health, it was difficult to persuade our low socioeconomic families about the benefits of eating well and exercising on their overall mental health. In my community garden, we had to transition kids with destructive tendencies into kids who began to nurture and support the growth of another living thing, while reaping the nutritional and mental health benefits of the gardening process. Changing the minds of people about naturally benefits them most has been an ongoing challenge but I remain more determined to educate on the benefits of holistic living.

What motivates you?

At my practice, we initially encounter individuals at their lowest and most vulnerable points in life. I am motivated to see the transformation in so many lives we touch. Their narratives are completely changed as they pursue their healthiest existence. Our outcomes are exceptional!

What is the three best qualities of your brand?

The unique approach to mental health treatment, focus on the well being of the entire family and its leadership.

Being an Entrepreneur is a 24/7 job, how do you balance that while being a family man?

I started a business so I could spend time with my family. Developing succinct process flows for every business function has allowed me to successfully be away from the business, while it continues to run seamlessly. I'm very proud of the automation controls that have led to successful operations when I'm away. And of course technology!

Where do you see yourself and your business in 10 years?

I'd like to establish wellness centers, all over the country that provides alternatives to mental health treatment that are natural and holistic.

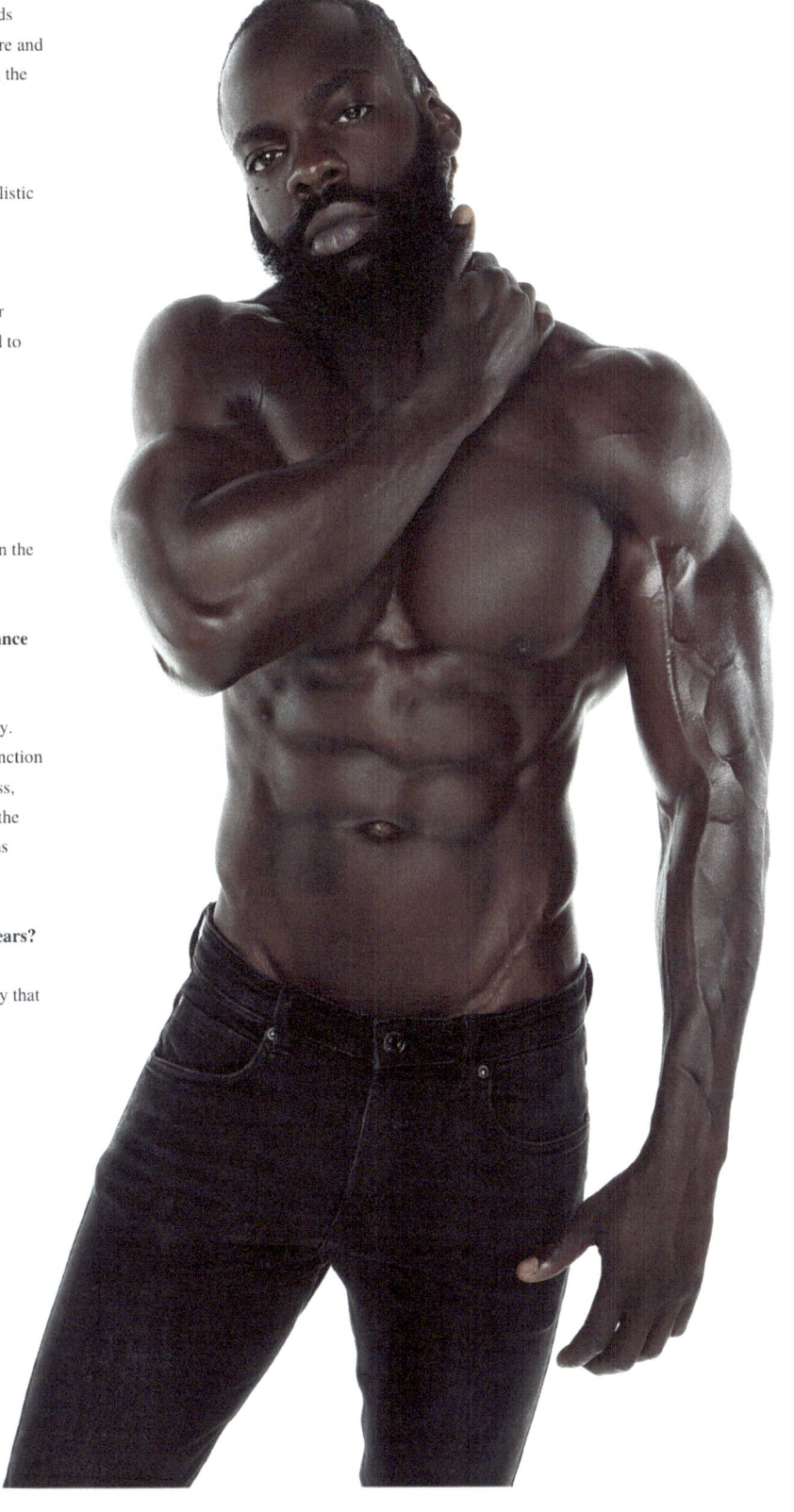

FASHION GXD MAGAZINE
FALL 2019 STAFF

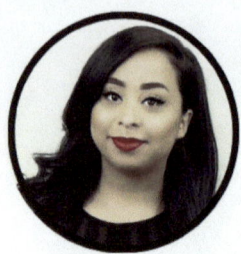

NYDIA FIGUEROA
lead makeup artist

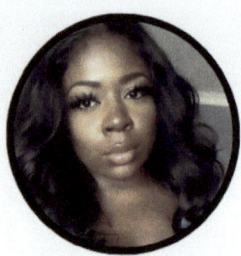

SHANTISE MICHELLE
lead hairstylist

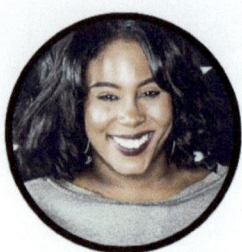

NOVIA ROSE
cover story / journalist

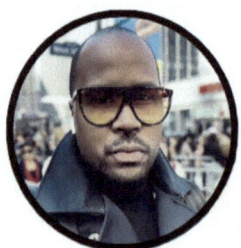

ANTOINE VON BOOZIER
editor / creative director

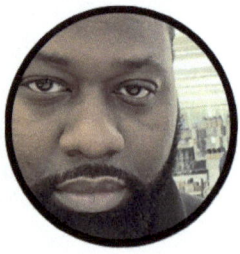

"NEZ" HARRIS
photographer / video

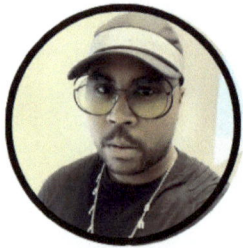

ANDRE VONBOOZIER
stylist / creative director

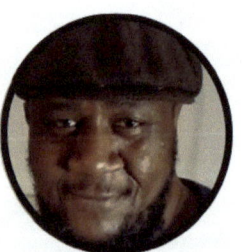

MELLO
photographer / full blossom magazine

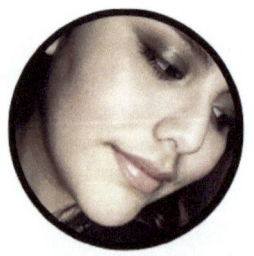

JOCELYN MIRANDA
assistant makeup artist

Fashion Gxd Magazine Designers

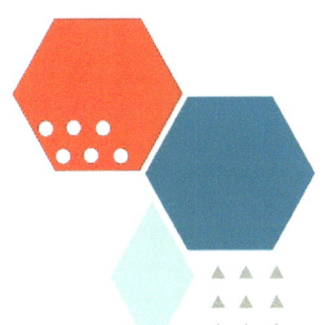

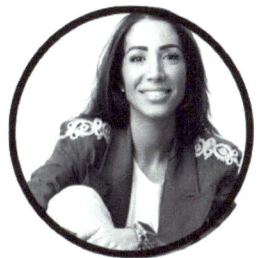

L2R LABEL
cover look designer

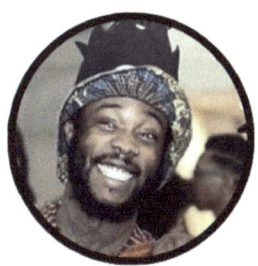

AFROOKLYN
designer

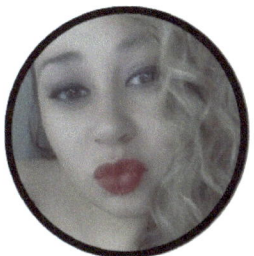

SHEENA HOC COTURE
designer

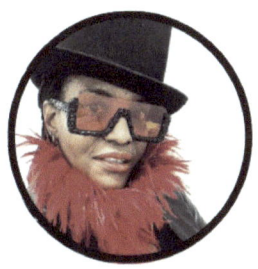

FUNK N CRYSTALS
eyewear designer

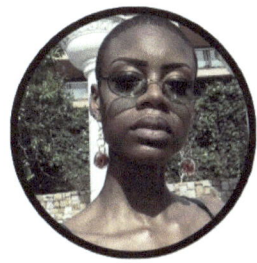

HEYTRANAE'
accessories

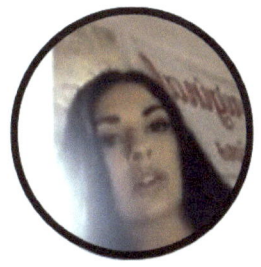

BREE BILLITER
designer/ accessories

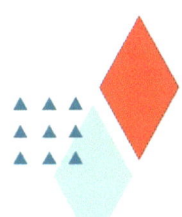

CANDICE'S

Snap Chat, Twitter, and Instagram @lilmissent. Follow Awesome Nobody on Twitter @awesomenobdy and Instagram @awesome_nobody17 YouTube channel The Little Miss Ent. Show-

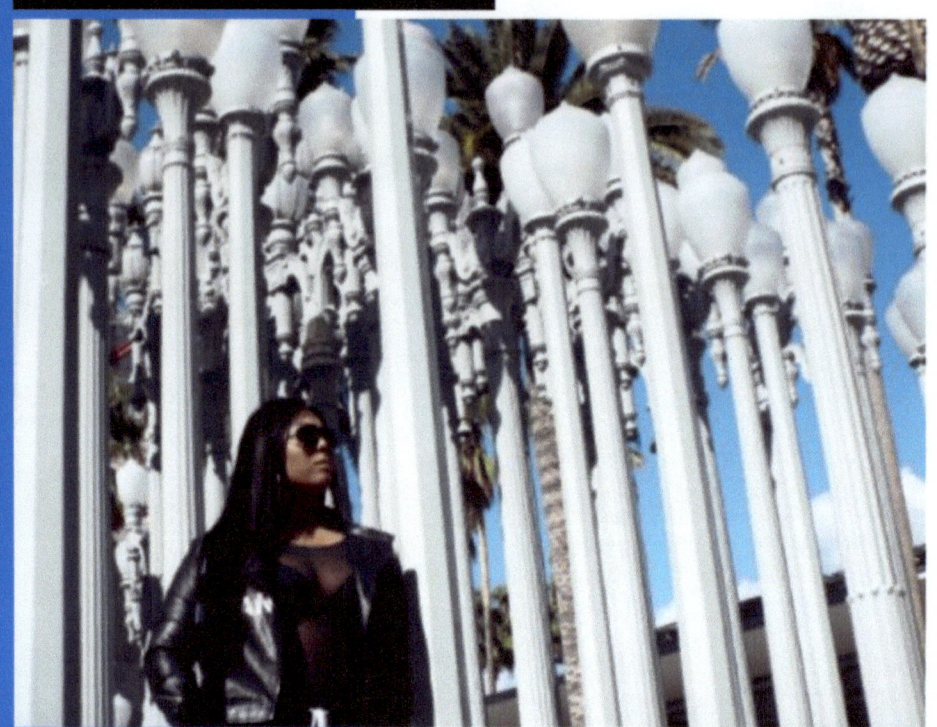

FIVE KEYS TO BEING A SUCCESSFUL PODCASTER

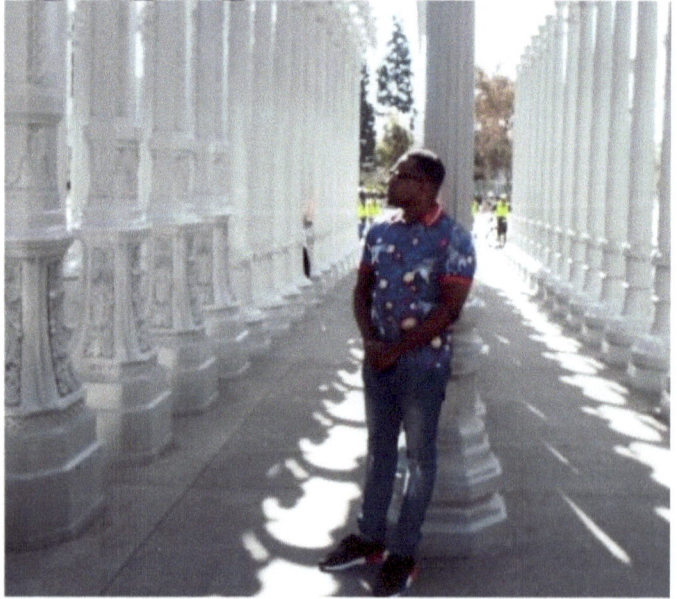

Candice is the host of The Little Miss Entertainment Show podcast. The podcast debut October 19th, 2015 and it is a must listen every Monday. Each show she interviews a guest. Her passion is allowing really amazing people to tell their really amazing story's. Also, her executive producer Awesome Nobody joins on their collaboration podcast "The Wedding Edition" documenting their recent engagement and planning their wedding together. Finally, catch the duo periodically on their spin off podcast "The Catch Up". During these episodes they share thoughts on Pop Culture, Music, and whatever the heck else is going on in the world.

Candice goes by the name Little Miss Entertainment because that is exactly what she is. She is a 10+ year executive in the entertainment business. She has worked with everyone from Kevin Hart to the late great Ms. Aretha Franklin.
In a recent interview Candice explains "It gives me such joy to be able to do things to put a smile on peoples faces. I love everything from throwing surprise birthday parties for my family members to putting on music festival for thousands of people. I love to create unforgettable moments for people" Between spending time with her family and traveling the world Candice wants to share all of her experiences through her podcast. Here are Candice's five tip t being a successful podcaster.

1.) BE YOURSELF. IT DOESN'T MATTER IF THERE ARE 1,000 INTERVIEW STYLE PODCAST, I KNOW THAT HOW I CONDUCT MY INTERVIEWS IS SPECIAL TO MY LISTENERS. THAT'S ALL THAT IS IMPORTANT. IF YOU TOUCH ONE OR ONE MILLION YOU'VE DONE YOUR JOB!

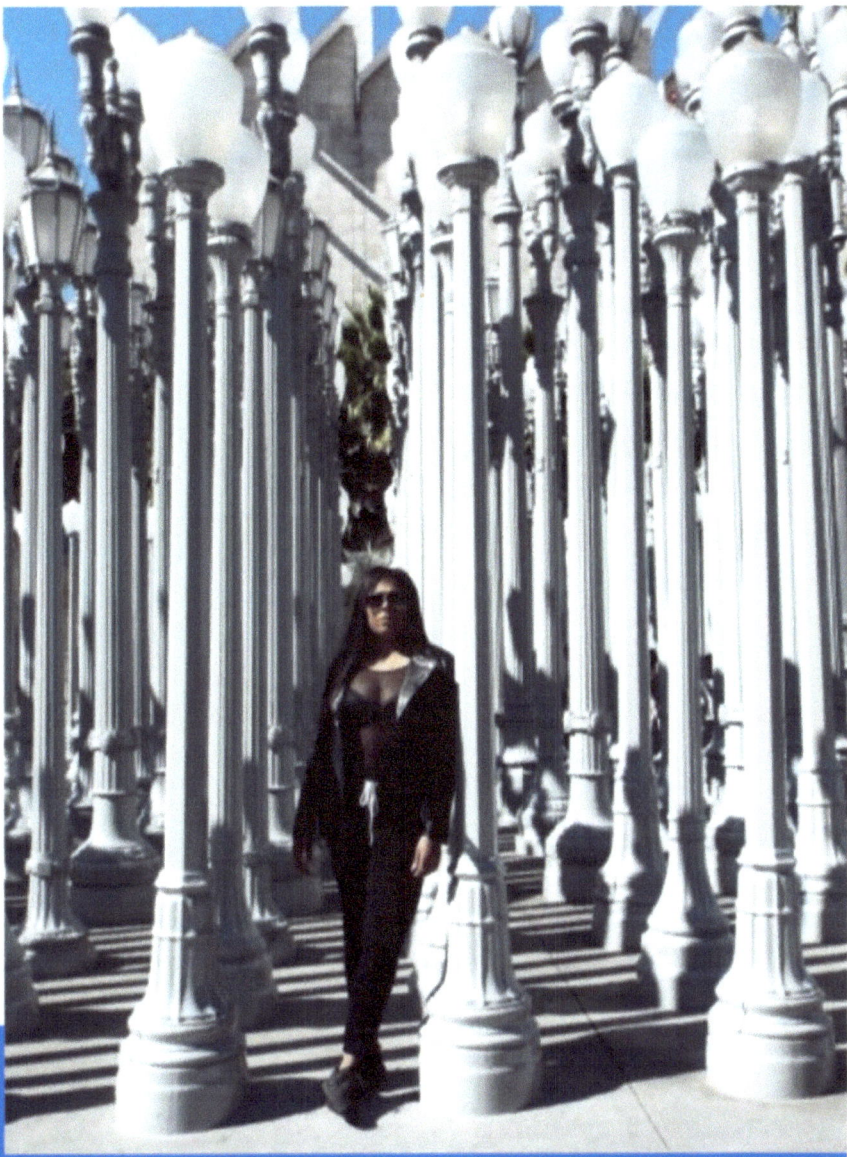

2.) Quality over quantity. Make great content that will last forever. A person should be able to binge your podcast from episode one and not think wow this is super dated. That doesn't mean don't talk about current events but, you should tie it back to something the listeners can learn from. Also, invest in good audio equipment. You don't have to break the bank to do so. Facebook market place is a gold mine for podcast equipment for cheap. Your listeners deserve to hear your content it is best form. Don't let them bed distracted by bad audio.

3.) Don't worry about the numbers. We live in a day in age where you can buy listens, followers, and likes. Don't worry about why you're not getting as many likes as the next podcast, worry about growing your brand awareness for other streams of revenue related to your podcast.

4.) Have merch! Podcast fans love to support and it's a great revenue stream. Also, wear your merch! You should be a walking billboard for your podcast. Be proud of what you created and broadcast it to the world. You never know who is watching. Also, support other podcast and they will support you too! It's nice to network with people with the same passion. If you see your fellow podcaster is selling merch to get money to book a venue to have a live podcast, support it! You will need that same support in return one day, trust me!

5.) Have an Executive Producer. It sounds fancier than it is but, it so important. Have a person that helps produce the show from a fresh set of eyes and different perspective. If you are the host you are a creative which in turns means you're a creative. And....creatives are sensitive about their work. You need someone to pick it apart and put it back together in its greatest form. I am blessed that my best friend, fiancé, and co-host Awesome Nobody is my Executive Producer. He is the engine that keeps the Little Miss Entertainment Show running. He schedules the interviews, edits the audio, researches the latest technology, maintains the YouTube channels, scouts the venues for the live shows, and DJs all our events. He is beyond amazing but, most importantly he sees the vision and he keeps me grounded. We are a team and every successful podcast needs a team!

Honorable Mention: Shout our your followers. My best friend Brittney told me once "Love Those Who Love You!" It was no truer words spoken. Your friends aren't your fans. They are people that love you for things outside of the podcast. They are bias. It's the person in your DM's from 5 states away your never met. They will tell you helped them through one of the toughest times in their life because they listen to your podcast today. That person deserves to be celebrated because that support is so real! I close everyone show by saying, I love you for listening because 100% you didn't have to." I mean that from my heart. My supporter are the reason I continue to challenge myself to be the best podcaster I can be.

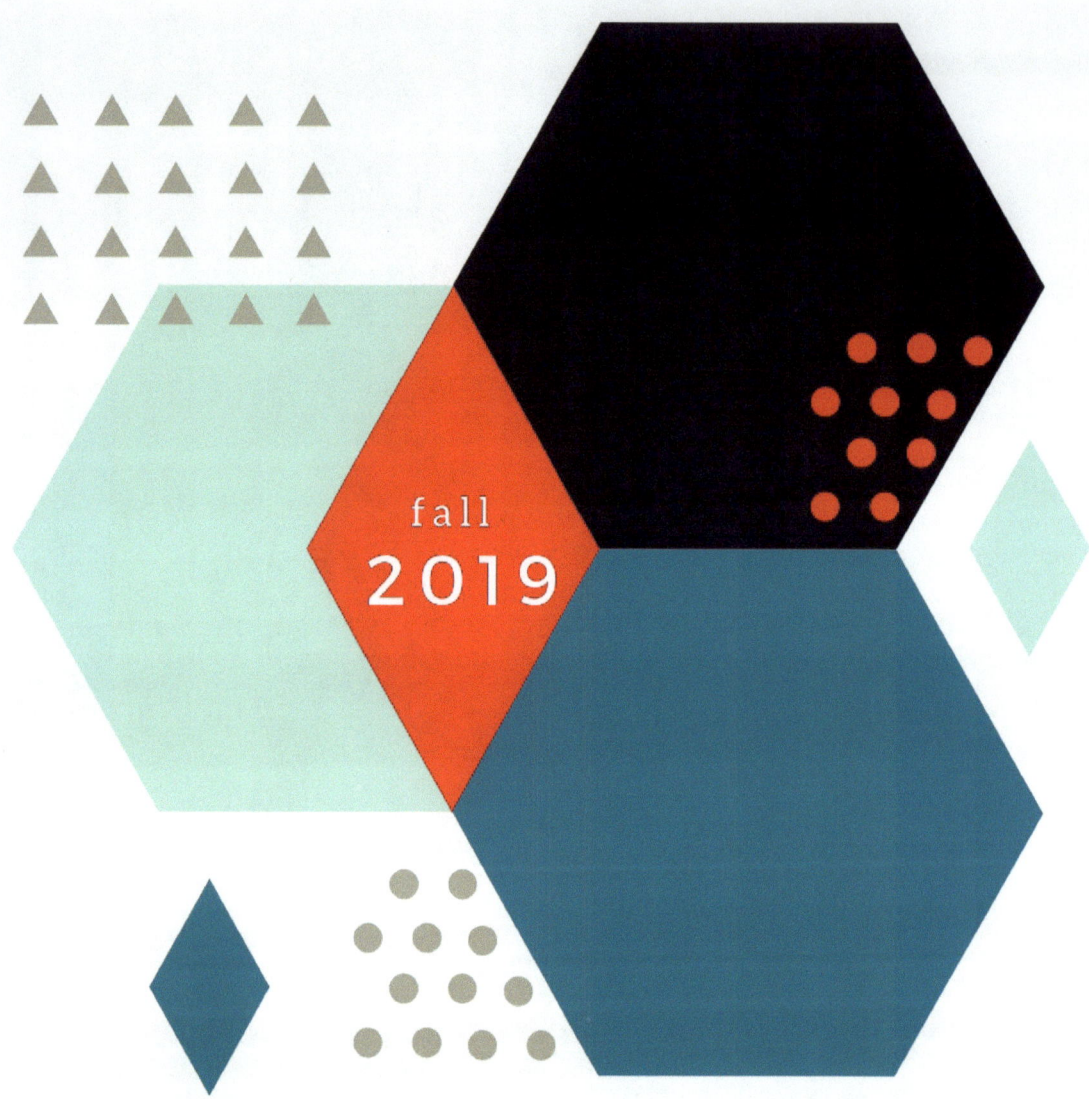

www.ingramcontent.com/pod-product-compliance
Lightning Source LLC
Chambersburg PA
CBHW040454220526
45473CB00004B/1637